Mahatma Gandhi
on
Moral Bankruptcy

About the Author

Dr. Anil Dutta Mishra is a distinguished Gandhian scholar and writer. He started his career as Assistant Professor in the Department of Non-violence and Peace Studies, Jain Vishva Bharati University, Ladnun, Rajasthan, became Deputy Director of National Gandhi Museum and Honorary Professor, Centre for Gandhian Philosophy and Human Development, Gayatri Vidya Parishad Degree College (Autonomous), Visakhapatnam and Treasurer, IIPA Delhi Regional Branch, New Delhi.

Dr. Mishra has held the post of General Secretary of Indian Society of Gandhian Studies, Alliance for Sarvodaya, Member Board of Studies, Nagpur and Punjab Universities and is Member of Gandhian Studies Centre of different colleges and universities across India sponsored by UGC. He has authored/edited 30 books and published a number of research papers. His recent book, *Reading Gandhi,* is widely acclaimed. Presently, he is Professor Research, Uttar Pradesh Rajarshi Tandon Open University, Allahabad, Uttar Pradesh.

MAHATMA GANDHI ON MORAL BANKRUPTCY

Anil Dutta Mishra

CONCEPT PUBLISHING COMPANY PVT. LTD.
NEW DELHI-110059

ISBN-13: 978-93-86682-43-7

First Published 2018

Published and Printed by:

Concept Since 1974

Concept Publishing Company Pvt. Ltd.
A/15-16, Commercial Block, Mohan Garden,
New Delhi-110059 (INDIA)
T : +91 11 25351460, +91 11 25351794
E : publishing@conceptpub.com, *W* : www.conceptpub.com

Cataloging in Publication Data--Courtesy: D.K. Agencies (P) Ltd. <docinfo@dkagencies.com>

Mishra, Anil Dutta, 1965- **author.**
Mahatma Gandhi on moral bankruptcy / Anii Dutta Mishra.
pages cm
Includes bibliographical references and index.
ISBN 9789386682437

1. Gandhi, Mahatma, 1869-1948—Ethics. 2. Social ethics—India. I. Title.

LCC DS481.G3M57 2018 DDC 170 23

Preface

Gandhi was really a great man in every sense. He was a creative philosopher, writer, warrior, institution builder, journalist and nationalist, *par excellence*. While leading humanity across the globe to fight against injustice, discriminatory laws, racial discrimination, Gandhi was also responding to the challenges coming in the way and always come up with unique methodology to overcome these challenges. The issues were contemporary, but its impact was everlasting and time tested. As a mass mobilizer he has to deal with number of issues concerning with human behaviour and its action. One of the issues that human being is confronting since its existence is that of *Kanchan* (*arth*) and *Kamini* (*kama*). Most of us are tempered to wealth and women. Wealth and women are natural attraction of human being. Wealth gives you power, prestige and through it you can have everything which you wish. In fact, wealth is not God, but it is also true that it is not less than God. Similarly, *Kama* is natural instinct of human being. It gives you ultimate pleasure, mental peace and is necessary for recreation. It is in fact union of souls. No pleasure is greater than pleasure of sexual intercourse under the restriction of *dharma*. Therefore, almost all our great saints lived a married life. Even a married one can lead a life of *brahmacharya*. Raja Janak is the best example. During struggle for *Swaraj*, Gandhi felt and observed that upholding ethics is necessary for country like India. He rightly said that British conquest of India is because of collapse of morality and ethics. So, time to time, Gandhi writes on the subject to re-establish morality at individual, societal and national level. Without transforming individual one cannot change the society and nation. One cannot transform India without transforming every Indian.

Gandhi was deep-rooted in Indian Culture and Civilization. He understood Indian Culture and Civilization and its downfall in-depth. His analysis and understanding was fundamental, unique and rare. He always questions the fundamentals. Gandhi placed morality at highest pedestrian. Morality is always a vital issue for the humanity. Morality is casuality in industrial and post-industrial society.

Gandhi published in 1926 in *Young India* under the title "Towards Moral Bankruptcy" in eight-part series. Whilst Gandhi was thinking of the problem and of the question of reading the literature on the subject, a book called *Towards Moral Bankruptcy* was placed in his hands for reading. It deals with this very subject and, as it appears to me, in a perfectly scientific manner. The original is in French by M. Paul Bureau and is entitled *L'Indiscipline des Moeurs* which literally means "the indiscipline of morals". The translation is published by Constable Company and has an introduction by Dr. Mary Scharlieb, C.B.E., M.D., M.S. (London). It covers 538 pages in 15 chapters. Gandhi had the habit of summarizing its main arguments and published them in his weekly newspaper.

Gandhi's approach was human-centric. He wrote and spoke on all aspects of life. After going through word-by-word of the *Collected Works of Mahatma Gandhi* (*CWMG*), I came to draw conclusion that even whole life is not enough to understand Mahatma Gandhi's thought, action and deed. For that one has to born and reborn again and again to understand him. He represents the continuum of Indian wisdom, culture and civilization.

This is most appropriate time when one can realize that Mahatma Gandhi's views which are more relevant than ever before or when he was alive.

To work on Mahatma Gandhi's any concept and its formulation is not an easy task. Collecting, researching materials on the subject from all Gandhiji's seventy writings, speeches and letters, representing his *sixty* years of very active public life is no easy task. To locate specific material from the *Collected Works of Mahatma Gandhi, Young India, Harijan, Navajivan*, D.G. Tendulkar's work etc. is also very difficult. It needs the thorough and deep understanding of Gandhi by the researcher.

Gandhi is now part of history and his words belong to humanity. There is vast literature on Gandhi, apart from his original works or compilation of his works, popularly known as *CWMG*, which are hundred bulky volumes is primary source. Original writing of Gandhi gives us the crystal clear understanding of the subject without any distortion. To make the book readers friendly it has been divided into two parts. In part one, an attempt has been made to present a broader debate on the subject keeping all the contemporary discourses and challenges in mind. In part two, Gandhi's original writings on Moral Bankruptcy is placed for reader's deeper understanding of the subject.

I am sure and hopeful, that the work will be worthwhile contribution on the subject with its immense current and future significance not only for Indian politicians and public servants but also for the others.

It is my pleasure to express my gratitude to a large number of people without whom this work would not have been possible. First and foremost, I would like to place my gratitude to Dr. Amrendra Kumar Dubey, IAS, Secretary, Ministry of Youth Affairs and Sports, Government of India, whose knowledge and thought always enlightened me. I would also like to thank my teachers, Professor Susheela Kaushik, Professor Manoranjan Mohanty, Professor Neera Chandhoke, Professor R.B. Jain and Professor M.P. Singh, all from University of Delhi and Professor M.S. Verma, Professor Prabhakar Pathak and Professor Bharti Srivastava of L.N.M.U., Bihar.

I cannot forget my friends, Mr. Prabhat Ranjan, IRTS, Mr. Atul Tiwari, IAS, Professor P.V. Sharma, Professor A.B.S.V. Ranga Rao, Professor Manohar Lal Sharma, Dr. Aditya Narayan Mishra and Dr. Kamal Srivastava who have always stood by me in all my academic endeavours.

I would also like to thank Shri T.N. Chaturvedi, former CAG and former Governor of Karnataka and Shri Subodh Kant Sahay, former Cabinet Minister, for their constant encouragements and blessings in all my academic pursuits. Another person, who greatly encouraged me, is Professor R.P. Misra, an eminent Gandhian and former Vice Chancellor, University of Allahabad.

Within the family, I am grateful to my wife, Dr. Sweta Mishra, and my pretty daughters, Sanstuti and Sansriti, for providing me peaceful environment to complete this work.

Last, but not the least, I take this opportunity to thank Shri Ashok Kumar Mittal, Managing Director, Concept Publishing Company Pvt. Ltd. for bringing out this volume in such a nice form and within record time.

15 November, 2017

Anil Dutta Mishra
anilduttamishra@gmail.com

Contents

PART ONE
INTRODUCTION

1
Introduction

To live a long, healthy and creative life, control over basic human instincts is essential, necessary and desirable in all circumstances and situations. Human being has a capacity to control its instincts and behaviour. Man by controlling the senses became different from other creatures. Control over senses makes a man healthy, worthy and wise. Control over senses is not an easy task. It requires pure heart, honesty, integrity, simple living and high thinking. Step-by-step, one can control the instincts. One can acquire real happiness through it but unfortunately, everyone is running after happiness through material pursuits and sexual desires. Happiness gained through uncontrolled material pursuits and sexual desires through unethical means lead to moral degradation of human being and through him in society and nation. From the time immemorial, all the saints and preachers talked about control of senses and laid stress to lead a simple life based on principle. Sensual instincts and attraction towards opposite sex are the basic parts of human behaviour and conduct. The challenge before human being is, how to tackle and control it? How to keep it in control of *dharma*? How to channelise that energy in proper direction to achieve the desired goal? How to follow the path of *brahmacharya* even in the married life or in the institution of marriage? Whole universe revolves around wants and desires are the manifestationss of culture and ideology, if they are given a free play then they lead to annihilation of moral values and culture. Path of social reform is very tough, the greatest challenge in front of human beings is to control the limitless passions and desires which are sucking the yogic aura and energy, and it is leading towards the depletion of supernatural energies gifted by nature.

Yoga never denies sex, but it tries to control the unchecked desires of sexual intercourse of human being mentally and physically. Most of the saints got married, they contributed in the social reform by setting an example through controlling the play of five senses. All the senses are sucking our life blood by distracting our attention from higher goals of life to attain *moksha* that is final liberation.

Gandhi himself led a life of self-control and pristine purity and he preached it for every aspect of human behaviour, be it social, be it political or be it economic. There should not be any dichotomy between private and public life. He experimented and preached. This book beautifully explores the various aspects of human life, spiritually and materialistically. Life is as you live or as you wish to live. Human being is a maker of his or her life. Life is a combination of joy and sorrow; pleasure and pain; ups and downs; name and defame. Life is colourful if you know to make it. Life is music if you know how to sing. Life is love and love is life. In fact, life is what not. Life is as you conceive or visualize it. Life is a combination of *yoga*, resistance and spirituality. Even before Gandhi, Swami Vivekananda too talked about the importance of self-restraint in life and travelled through different areas related to morality. He rightly said that learning should revolve around morality and character building. The main focus in learning is to make the hidden ability of a learner manifest. As Vivekananda said, "what a man 'learns' is really what he 'discovers', by taking the cover off his own soul, which is a mine of infinite knowledge." As per the Vedantic philosophy, knowledge is inherent in a human being, like a spark in a piece of flint, and all that is needed is the strike of suggestion to bring it out. 'Manifestation' indicates spontaneous growth, provided that the impediments, if any, are removed. Vivekananda said: "The education which does not help the common mass of people to equip themselves for the struggle for life, which does not bring out strength of character, a spirit of philanthropy, and the courage of a lion – it is worth the name? Real education is that which enables one to stand on one's own legs."

Education, he said, must provide "life-building, man-making, character-making assimilation of ideas". The ideal of this type of education would be to produce an integrated person – one who has learned how to improve his intellect, purify his emotions, and stand firm on moral virtues and unselfishness. The external and internal obstacles, if any, are removed at the proper time by the teachers or the education system. In order to tackle these obstacles, the education system should take on two responsibilities: (i) it should help a person build a healthy and dynamic frame of mind to enable him to meet the challenges of life; and (ii) it should try to prevent, through proper training of its present students, any future evils in people and society which are likely to further complicate the problems of human beings. At the same time, however, the teachers and the designers of education systems must always keep in mind the Vedantic idea that whatsoever good or bad impressions a mind carries, a human being is essentially pure and divine, and a repository of immense possibilities.

As the tortoise tucks its feet and head inside the shell, and you may kill it and break it in pieces, and yet it will not come out, even so the character of that man who has control over his motives and organs is unchangeably established. He controls his own inner forces, and nothing can draw them out against his will. By this continuous reflex of good thoughts, good impressions moving over the surface of the mind, the tendency for doing well becomes strong, and as the result we feel able to control the *Indriyas* (the sense-organs, the nerve-centres). Thus alone will character be established, and then alone a man gets to truth. In order to achieve true liberation, it is important to control all mental desires and tendencies to enjoy sense pleasures.

Saints since time immemorial, talked about spiritual love. Spiritual love or *brahmacharya* before marriage and even after marriage leads to divinity. *Bhakti* movement poets talked about spiritual love that is beyond the chains of sensual and bodily pleasures. Life is full of challenges, if we are controlled by passions. The best example is Mira Bai. She calls her body unimportant. She danced on the music of the soul and she never gave importance to the bodily pleasures. She loved the soul and her soul was directly related to Lord, she always tried to fulfil the needs of her soul. Soul never demands the religious discussions and intellectual talks. Body is only the medium through which we can meet God. It has come from dust and in dust it will be dashed. So, there is no need to worship body, but we should worship Krishna.

Meaningful life has become a dream due to the uncontrolled desires and pleasures. Building of true character needs an indomitable spirit. Awareness of spiritual goals will help youngsters prominently to resist the damaging enticements of drugs, delinquency and promiscuous sex. As Gandhi beautifully wrote about *brahmacharya* in *Harijan*, 15-6-1947, "The outward behaviour of a man is at once the sign and proof of the inner state. He who has killed the sexual urge in him will never be guilty of it in any shape or form. However, attractive a woman may be, her attraction will produce no effect on the man without the urge. The same rule applies to woman ... *Brahmacharya* is not a virtue that can be cultivated by outward restraints. He who runs away from a necessary contact with a woman does not understand the full meaning of *Brahmacharya* ... The true *Brahmacharya* will shun false restraints. He must create his own fences according to his limitations, breaking them down when he feels that they are unnecessary. The first thing is to know what true *Brahmacharya* is, then to realize its value and lastly to try to cultivate this priceless virtue. I hold that true service of the country demands this observance."

In one context, *Brahmacharya* is the first of four *Ashramas* of human life, with *Grihastha*, *Vanaprastha* and *Sannyasa* being the other three *ashramas*. Every *ashrama* is prelude of other and its time span is 25 years. The *Brahmacharya* stage of one's life, up to 25 years of age, was focused on learning and included the practice of celibacy. This is the stage when a man practices *yoga* and attains knowledge. Indian traditions, it connotes discipline and innocence during the student stage of life for the purposes of learning from a *guru*, and during later stages of life for the purposes of attaining spiritual liberation. *Brahmacharya* is a virtue, where it means celibacy when unmarried, and fidelity when married. The second stage is *Grihastha*. In this stage one can experiment what they learn in *Brahmacharya* stage for individual and society within the purview of *dharma*. This is a stage of creation and preparation for third stage. The third stage is devoted to *Vanaprastha.* In this stage you are doing for community and society. The fourth stage is *Sannyasa.* Here, one belongs to entire world. No property, no attachment, no sexual pleasure. Devote time for ultimate goal of human being that is complete liberation to attain *Moksha.* Man and his action are for entire world. He lives like a saint. The concept of *purushartha* has three related meanings. First, it means any human striving; secondly, it refers to human striving directed towards overcoming fate and *karma.* And thirdly, it refers to any one of the four canonically recognized aims of life, viz., *dharma* (ethics and religion), *artha* (wealth and power), *kama* (pleasure) and *moksha* (liberation from *samsara,* the cycle of birth, death and rebirth).

In present context, spirituality emphasizes humanistic qualities such as love, compassion, patience, tolerance, forgiveness, contentment, responsibility, harmony, and a concern for others, aspects of life and human experience which go beyond a purely materialist view of the world, without necessarily accepting belief in a supernatural reality or divine being. Spiritual practices such as mindfulness and meditation can be experienced as beneficial or even necessary for human fulfilment without any supernatural interpretation or explanation. Spirituality in this context may be a matter of nurturing thoughts, emotions, words and actions that are in harmony with a belief that everything in the universe is mutually dependent; this stance has much in common with some versions of Buddhist spirituality. One may define it as: "Spirituality exists wherever we struggle with the issues of how our lives fit into the greater scheme of things. This is true when our questions never give way to specific answers or give rise to specific practices such as prayer or meditation. We encounter spiritual issues every time we wonder where the universe comes from, why we are here, or what happens when we die. We also become spiritual when we become moved by values such as beauty, love, or creativity that seem to reveal a meaning or power beyond our visible world. An idea or practice is 'spiritual' when it reveals our personal desire to establish a felt-relationship with the deepest meanings or powers governing life."

Whilst the terms *spirituality* and *religion* both relate to a search for an Absolute or God, and thus have much overlap, there are also characteristic differences in their usage. Religion implies a particular faith tradition that includes acceptance of a metaphysical or supernatural reality; whereas spirituality is not necessarily bound to any particular religious tradition.

Mahatma Gandhi was a highly spiritual person in thought, action and deeds. His spiritualism was part of the daily life. Gandhi's life synthesized spirituality and political activism. Gandhi believed in human dignity and freedom; he fought injustice with words, ideals, and self-discipline. Gandhi's unique philosophy helped free India and influenced generations of peace activists. Throughout his life, Gandhi remained committed to non-violence and truth even in the most extreme situations. He lived simply, organizing an *ashrama* that was self-sufficient in its needs. Making his own clothes — the traditional Indian *dhoti* and *shawl* woven with a *charkha*, he lived on a simple vegetarian diet. He used rigorous fasts, for long periods, for both self-purification and protest.

An important spiritual goal pursued by Gandhi was austerity, particularly based on control of bodily appetites. As a young man, Gandhi began using food in experiments to test his willpower: "As I searched myself deeper, the necessity for changes both internal and external began to grow on me . . . I saw that the writers on vegetarianism had examined the question very minutely, attacking it in its religious, scientific, practical, and medical aspects." The test of his willpower and subsequent control of his will were disciplines that Gandhi cultivated in himself for the rest of his life. Later, this same austerity helped Gandhi to lead his people by example.

Gandhi's curiosity and his desire to understand and improve himself led him to spend hours studying religious books and contemplating philosophical ideas. He found the *Bhagavad Gita*, the sacred text of the Hindus, especially inspiring. This text contain lessons in discipline and selflessness, mercifulness, and freedom from greed or jealousy. Yet certain aspects of Hinduism did not appeal to Gandhi. He rejected the notion that to be devout meant to live quietly, meditating as some mystic Hindus did. Instead, Gandhi felt the need to do act with a pure mind.

He beautifully integrated and harmonized the values of *artha* and *moksha*, secularism and spirituality, power and justice. *Purusharthas*, as interpreted by Gandhi, provide a set of values and ideals within which public discourse in India should be conducted. He presents a balanced view of life. Wealth, power, pleasure, aesthetic beauty, ethical integrity and freedom of the spirit, the *purusharthas*, are goals that all Indians seek. Gandhi explains how and why that seeking should be the basis of modern India's public philosophy.

Gandhi himself beautifully sumsup, he alone is religious, he alone is happy and he alone is wealthy, who is sincere in himself, bears no malice, exploits no one and always acts with a pure mind. Such man alone can serve mankind.

If we sustain a perfect equilibrium between our spiritual and material life, we can keep discontent and unhappiness at bay.

There is a strong correlation between the two. Spiritualism also has a material essence. Spirituality does not mean renunciation of worldly affairs. The source of spiritual life is self-realization and once we realize inner self our vision becomes clear to achieve happiness and peace.

Gandhi believes in controlling the senses through the medium of *yoga* as manifested in *Vedas* and scriptures. According to the *Sankhya* philosophy, nature is composed of three forces called *Sattva*, *Rajas*, and *Tamas*. These as manifested in the physical world are what we may call equilibrium, activity, and inertness. *Tamas* is typified as darkness or inactivity; *Rajas* is activity, expressed as attraction or repulsion; and *Sattva* is the equilibrium of the two. "*Karma Yoga* has specially to deal with these three factors. By teaching what they are and how to employ them, it helps us to do our work better." Human society is a graded organization. We all know about morality, and we all know about duty, but at the same time we find that in different countries the significance of morality varies greatly. What is regarded as moral in one country may in another be considered perfectly immoral. For instance, in one country cousins may marry; in another, it is thought to be very immoral; in one, men may marry their sisters-in-law; in another, it is regarded as immoral; in one country people may marry only once; in another, many times; and so forth. Similarly, in all other departments of morality, we find the standard varies greatly—yet we have the idea that there must be a universal standard of morality. Gandhi says that every activity should revolve around morality. He defines true love and gives importance to spirituality as the essence of life. Krishna says, "Look at Me, Arjuna! If I stop from work for one moment, the whole universe will die. I have nothing to gain from work; I am the one Lord, but why do I work? Because I love the world." God is unattached because He loves; that real love makes us unattached. Wherever there is attachment, the clinging to the things of the world, you must know that it is all physical attraction between sets of particles of matter—something that attracts two bodies nearer and nearer all the time and, if they cannot get near enough, produces pain; but where there is real love, it does not rest on physical attachment at all. Such lovers may be a thousand miles away from one another, but their love will be all the same; it does not die, and will never produce any painful reaction.

Bhaktivedanta mentioned that, "With the body, with the mind, with the intellect, even merely with the senses, the *Yogis* perform action toward self-purification, having abandoned attachment. He who is disciplined in *Yoga*, having abandoned the fruit of action, attains steady peace..."

We are a mass of happiness or misery; we have seen that hundreds of times in our lives. As a rule, the young are optimistic and the old pessimistic. The young have life before them; the old complain their days are gone; hundreds of desires, which they cannot fulfil, struggle in their hearts. Both are foolish nevertheless. Life is good or evil according to the state of mind in which we look at it, it is neither by itself. Fire, by itself, is neither good nor evil. When it keeps us warm we say, "How beautiful is fire!" When it burns our fingers, we blame it. Still, in itself it is neither good nor bad. According as we use it, it produces in us the feeling of good or bad; so also is this world.

Control of senses is at the base of Gandhi's philosophy, he gives importance to celibacy. Control comprises various aspects; it is not related to sex only, but trustworthy behaviour towards companion too. Gandhi says that morality is not related to abstaining sex, but it is related to get rid of free play of sexual impulses without resistance. Gandhi is against the use of contraceptives because it encourages immorality. Control of senses is the control of animal passion and it can be controlled only through character building. Celibacy controls all the sense organs. All the five senses control human mind and souls and man runs after sensual pleasures and he never attains fulfilment. Every sensual pleasure attracts him and traps him. For transient excitement man loses his spiritual vigour and energy. If one sense organ is controlled, then all other senses fall into respective places. Gandhi follows the path of truth, non-violence and *brahmacharya*. He talks about the control of senses after marriage. Marriage does not give the right to do sex anytime, but it teaches the path of control, he himself mentions about his personal experience: "From that day when I began *Brahmacharya*, our freedom began. My wife became a free woman, free from my authority as her lord and master, and I became free from the slavery to my own appetite, which she had to satisfy. No other woman had any attraction for me in the same sense that my wife had. I was too loyal to her as husband and too loyal to the vow I had taken before my mother to be slave to any other woman. But the manner in which my *Brahmacharya* came to me irresistibly drew me to woman as the mother of man. She became too sacred for sexual love. And so every woman at once became sister or daughter to me."

One specific way contraceptives negatively affect a marital relationship, according to Bedford, is through the demeaning of spouses due to the fulfilment solely of sexual desires. When sex is justified because "we are not going to get pregnant", it dehumanizes one's spouse. It ignores the needs of the other spouse in order to fulfil one's own desires. It lowers the value of the other person by putting one's desires above that of the spouse. This is outside God's will for the way that married couples should treat one another.

Physical fulfilment and satisfaction through sexual intercourse ultimately leads to spiritual union. Firstly bodies are united then physical attraction annihilates and spiritual journey begins. Gandhi reacts against the use of contraceptives, he says that a man should face the consequences of his actions; running away from one's responsibility is a sin. Man should rise above sexual intercourse for the purpose of carnal satisfaction: "God has blessed man with seed that has the highest potency and woman with a field richer than the richest earth to be found anywhere on this globe. Surely, it is criminal folly for man to allow his most precious possession to run to waste. He must guard it with a care greater than he will bestow upon the richest pearls in his possession. And so is a woman guilty of criminal folly who will receive the seed in her life-producing field with the deliberate intention of letting it run to waste. Both he and she will be judged guilty of misuse of the talent given to them and they will be dispossessed of what they have been given."

In *Harijan*, 5-5-1946 Gandhi wrote that use of contraceptives degrades woman status and they are seen as sexual objects. The difference between a prostitute and a woman using contraceptives is only this that the former sells her body to several men, the latter sells it to one man. Man has no right to touch his wife so long as she does not wish to have a child, and the woman should have the will-power to resist even her own husband. Further, Gandhi mentions in Chapter V of *Towards Moral Bankruptcy*:

> "All men and young men in particular, can experience the immediate benefit of chastity. The memory is quiet and tenacious, the brain lively and fertile, the will energetic, the whole character gains a strength of which libertines have no conception; no prism shows us our surroundings under such heavenly colours as that of chastity, which lights up with its rays the least objects in the universe, and transports us into the purest joys of an abiding happiness that knows neither shadow nor decline." And the author adds: "The joy, the cordial merriment, the sunny confidence of vigorous young men who have remained chaste . . . are an eloquent contrast to the restless obsessions and feverish excitement of their companions who are slaves to the demands of sensuality." He then compares the benefits of chastity with "the miserable consequences of lust and debauchery". "No disease", the author states, "could ever be quoted as the result of continence; who is not aware of the frightful diseases of which moral indiscipline is the source?" "The body ... finds itself

> converted into an indescribable state of rottenness ... Nor can we forget the worse defilement of imagination, heart and understanding. On every side we hear complaint of the lowering of the character, the unbridled lust of youth, the overflowing of selfishness."

Gandhi rejects the idea of taking contraceptive because a female is treated as an object to play, she is treated as a prostitute. Woman is a cultural construct and our scriptures give important place to her. It is a challenge for modern society to retain that divine status. Females have been following the image of Sati, Sita and Savitri since times immemorial. The Indian woman with the inner strength of godly virtues survives all the odds. She struggles throughout her life to survive and not to live. The thesis challenges the domination of patriarchal thought in which men claim to define what is good for woman or what is not without consulting them. Indian women have consciously accepted the supremacy of the patriarchal value system by surrendering meekly to the traditionally assigned roles and allowing themselves to be dominated. Simone de Beauvoir puts it in the book '*The Second Sex*' that, "The culture that created Sita and a Gandhari has denied existence to woman except as a daughter/sister, a wife/daughter-in-law, and a mother/mother-in-law. The Hindu society has denied woman the possibility of being a "SHE, a person capable of achieving individuation ... So, the women of today are in a fair way to dethrone the myth of femininity; they are beginning to affirm their independence in concrete ways; but they do not easily succeed in living completely the life of a human being. Reared by women within a feminine world, their normal destiny is marriage, which still means practically subordination to man."

Gandhi says that one of the issues that human beings are confronting since its existence is that of *Kanchan* (*arth*) and *Kamini* (*kama*). Most of us are tempered to wealth and women. Wealth and women are natural attraction of man. The Indian women with the inner strength of godly virtues survives all the odds. She struggles throughout her life to survive and not to live. The thesis challenges the domination of patriarchal thought in which men claim to define what is good for woman or what is not without consulting them.

Myths should be revised, rewritten, and retold from a feministic point of view, feministic discourse is different from the male discourse, especially by contrasting myths from the *Mahabharata* with stories from the Sanskrit. Gandhi says that contraceptives should be avoided by married and unmarried both because married females should have control upon the senses and unmarried women are treated as prostitutes if they are sexually harassed and molested due to the option of birth control, marriage becomes an instrument of female exploitation and subjugation. Myths should be reanalyzed, rewritten and retold from the feminine perspective. Patriarchal assumptions of original tales should be interrogated; *Mahabharata* should be analysed from the feministic perspective telling not of Karna, Arjuna or Bhima, but of Gandhari and Amba. Every myth, in the name of religion exhibits women's suppression. Survival is the highest ideal in the struggle ridden life of women. The old myths are eroded, new woman-centred myths are needed to be formed to ask questions, seek answers and reconstruct power-structure.

Gandhari keeps her faith intact in the moral order and in the hours of supreme crisis in her life, she always unhesitatingly sacrifices her narrow, personal, selfish interests, and embraces the cause of virtue and righteousness. Gandhari, as soon as she knows that her husband is blind, makes up her mind to voluntarily deny herself the pleasure of eyesight by wrapping her eyes with thick bandage. She keeps that bandage on her eyes throughout her life and sees the world through the pure light of sacrifice and devotion for her husband. The question arises is it her devotion for her husband or the manifestation of anger to know about the blindness of her husband? As a wife, Draupadi became the ideal mistress of the household when Yudhishthira became installed as a king. She was a woman possessing courage and sense of dignity. When Yudhishthira lost her in the game of dice at Hastinapur, and Duhshasana, brother of Duryodhana, taking recourse to unfair means, heaped all sorts of personal insult upon her in the open assembly. As a faithful wife, she accompanied the *Pandavas* in their journey to the forest. Similarly, Sita in *Ramayana* accompanied her husband in the dark stages of life, but she had to give "*Agni Pariksha*".

Gandhi talks about honesty and truth in marriage. Our epics also represent the ideal image of women, when Sita is brought before Rama, then Rama tells that she has stained herself by staying in another person's abode and therefore, he would like to renounce her and asks her to choose to live either with Lakshmana or Vibhishana or Sugriva. Sita, after hearing the cruel speech of Rama, trembles and weeps with heavy tears, and she is ashamed before that great assembly. However, she wipes out the tears from her face and tells Rama that she can prove her purity. Then she turns towards Lakshmana and tells that with such an insult she would not wish to live in this world and asks him to prepare a funeral pyre for her. Then Lakshmana turns towards Rama and finding him silent, he prepares the funeral pyre. Sita exemplifies the cardinal virtues of women, devotion, dedication and subservience.

To the extent that most religious people have based their faith on mere dogmas imbibed from their culture, and because their perspective on spiritual issues is skewed by their presuppositions, they often misinterpret the true nature of their experience.

Furthermore, most people make the mistake of being outward-directed, living under the sway of external objects. If they could learn to look within, they would find the answers of many of their religious questions and longings within their own spiritual nature. "The man who thinks that he is receiving a response to his prayers does not know that the fulfilment comes from his own nature, that he has succeeded, by the mental attitude of prayer, in waking-up a bit of this infinite power which is coiled-up within himself. *Raja Yoga* is the science of religion, the rationale of all worship, all prayers, forms, ceremonies, and miracles". Vivekananda distinguishes among three levels of the mind or psyche: the unconscious mind, which consists of one's instinctive urges and desires; the conscious mind, which is self-aware, but still driven by selfishness, ambition, and greed; and the super conscious mind, which comes from the highest source of spiritual reality, namely the supreme *Brahman-Atman* or *Purusha*.

Raja Yoga is divided into eight steps. These steps are: *Yama, Niyama, Asana, Pranayama, Pratyahara, Dharana, Dhyana* and *Samadhi*. *Yama*: the vows of abstention, including non-killing of sentient beings, refraining from lying, refraining from stealing, moderating one's physical desires, and refusing to accept gifts. *Niyama*: the positive precepts, whereby one keeps oneself clean both physically and mentally, has a contented and cheerful attitude, develops good habits in one's study of *yoga*, and devotes oneself wholly to God. *Asana*: the discipline of good posture when meditating, holding the back erect and keeping the chest, neck, and head in a straight line. *Pranayama*: the control of the *prana* energy, which according to Hindu philosophy connects the individual with the rest of the universe. The starting point of *pranayama* is breath control, but it involves also the heartbeat and the flow of all one's psycho-spiritual energies. *Pratyahara*: the internalization of perception (literally, it means a "gathering toward", whereby one detaches the mind from the externality of objects and experiences them rather as functions of one's own awareness. In other words, one still perceives objects, but no longer thinks of them as "out there", separate from oneself. *Dharana*: forcibly holding the attention fixed on a single object of experience, to the exclusion of any others. Since, one has already mastered *pratyahara* at this stage, however, the one-pointedness is not outwardly, but inwardly directed, usually toward one of the *chakras*. In so doing, one is really focusing on the mind itself as it keeps hold of a fixed center of awareness. *Dhyana*: that is, total concentration, conferring such mastery of the thought-waves that one can direct them in an unbroken current towards any object, external or internal. In effect, one has learned how to enter the trance state at will. *Samadhi*: the supreme bliss of enlightenment, in which the mind achieves a super conscious state of objectless contemplation. This is the ultimate goal of all religion, according to Vivekananda.

Due to moral degradation and the free play of senses, society is leading towards decline. On one hand, ours is considered to be a spiritual nation. On the other hand, we live in a society where women are treated very badly. Girls are so unwanted that millions are aborted in the womb or killed right after birth. After they are born, they struggle through a childhood in which they are second class citizens. Young girls are deprived of the same opportunities their brothers receive.

Gandhi is against the birth control by chemical and mechanical means. He says: It removes all sensible motives for self-control and makes it possible for sexual indulgence in marriage to be limited only by the dwindling of yearning. Apart from this, however, it inevitably has an influence outside the marriage relation. It opens the door for uneven, licentious and unproductive unions, which from the point of view of modern industry, sociology and politics are full of immorality. Contraception is leading to sexual indulgence both in and out of marriage. The birth of a human being is a great science, and therefore, reformation of the act of copulation according to the Vedic ritual called *Garbhadhana-samskara* is vital for generating good population. Our focus should not be to check the growth of the population, but to generate good population on the level of Vidura, Vyasa and Janaka whose life stories we are all familiar with. Then the so-called birth control is not only vicious, but also useless. That is why religions are against abortion. Religion and scriptures are against abortions and contraceptives, they give the instruction of the control of senses and natural sex in institution of marriage only. Values should be ingrained in the children if they are born through immoral means and illegal sex then it leads to inhuman population. The conditions for having good progeny in society are that the husband should be disciplined in religious and regulative principles and the wife should be faithful to the husband. "In the wake of abortion," says M. Bureau, "come infanticide, incest, and crimes that outrage nature. There is nothing special to say about the first, except that the crime has become more frequent in spite of all the facilities offered to unmarried mothers and of the extension of anti-conceptionist practices and abortion. It no longer arouses the same reprobation among so-called respectable people, and juries usually return a verdict of 'not guilty'."

In *The Bhagavadgita* it is said that sexual intercourse according to religious principles is a divine act. Krishna says *Bhuteshukamosmi*—I am lust (*Kama*) among beings. Lust with proper application was a virtue and not a sin and that is what Krishna means. Before engaging in sexual intercourse, both the husband and the wife must consider their mental condition, the particular time, the husband's direction, and obedience to the demigods.

According to Vedic society, there is a suitable auspicious time for sex life, which is called the time for *garbhadhana*; personalities like Ravana and Hiranyakashipu were actually born of *Brahmanas*, but they were not accepted as *Brahmanas* because their fathers did not follow the moral principles for their birth. Such children are called devils. During the age of *Kali* there is no discipline in sex life. How, then, can one expect good children? Certainly unwanted children cannot be a source of happiness in society, but they can be raised to the human standard by spiritual outlook and upbringing. Vidura though born as an illegitimate unwanted child was brought up with discipline who later became a legal expert on social matters.

Children are to be brought up to respect the law of celibacy, of continence, until they are actually married, so, the husband and the wife should adhere to the law of continence and celibacy; and for them, this law should operate in the form of a strict moderation of marital life. Marital life should be based upon self-control, not upon indulgence. Then, the wife should regard the husband as the only partner and *vice versa*. The wife should not have any other male and she should not think of any other man, but should be devoted to her husband; no thought of any other man should ever cross her mind. All the rest of humanity should be to her like children—she is the great Mother. The husband must have the vow which Rama had—the vow of the single spouse. That means that the thought of another woman will never enter his mind. To him, the only woman is his wife and their marriage ties are sacred. In this way, the whole family set-up becomes sacred and holy and the interior life of the spirit goes on unhampered. There is nothing in the exterior life of the being to injure the spiritual life. There is nothing in the exterior life—either in the family life or in one's personal life to hold back or obstruct the spiritual life.

Ideals of motherhood, monogamy, chastity, heterosexuality, sexual harassment, practices of gynaecology, obstetrics, and psychotherapy, unpaid labour and, overt violence: rape, sexual abuse, prostitution, incest, hysterectomies and pornography, all are parts of patriarchy. The main motive of feminism is to defeat patriarchy through consciousness rising.

Gandhi says that religion may not be taken in its narrow, parochial sense. True religion is the greatest disturbing factor in life, whether individual or collective. A religious awakening constitutes a revolution, a transformation, regeneration. Our religion is based upon scriptures and religious books. The path of social reform, like the path of heaven, is strewn with numerous difficulties.

Periyar E.V. Ramasamy, founder of the Iconoclastic Self-Respect Movement, was highly critical of the given notions of masculinity and argued that except for the fact of giving birth and nursing the infant in the early months, there is nothing that distinguishes women from men: neither in the realm of emotions, nor in the area of rational thought. Yet women were deemed subordinate, valued chiefly for their sexual allure and ability to bear children. This was because masculinity set the laws and arranged the world to the advantage of men, a historical development with immense consequences for women.

Beauvoir in her book, *The Second Sex* wrote that one is not born, but rather becomes a woman. No biological, no psychological, or economic fate determines the figure that the human female presents the society; it is civilization as a whole that produces the creature intermediate between male and eunuch, which is described as feminine.

Beauvoir argues that women have historically been considered deviant, abnormal. She says that even Mary Wollstonecraft considered men to be the ideal toward which women should aspire. Beauvoir said that this attitude limited women's success by maintaining the perception that they were a deviation from the normal, and were always outsiders attempting to emulate "normality." She opines that woman's idea of herself as inferior to man and dependent on him springs from her realization that the world is masculine on the whole. Everything helps to confirm this hierarchy in the eyes of little girl. The historical and literary culture to which she belongs, the songs and legends, with which she lulled to sleep, are one long exaltation of man. Beauvoir asserts that women are as capable of choice as men, and thus, can choose to elevate themselves, moving beyond the 'immanence' to which they were previously resigned and reaching 'transcendence,' a position in which one takes responsibility for oneself and the world, where one chooses one's freedom.

The concept of 'other' brings to mind the 'second sex,' the oppressed women. It depicts the tension rising from the female characters' struggle against patriarchy (Millet, *Sexual Politics*). Beauvoir in the book *The Second Sex* acknowledges this fact when she says: "Since patriarchal times, women have, in general forced to occupy a secondary place in the world in relation to men ... in spite of the fact that women constitute numerically at least half of the human race, and the secondary standing is not imposed of necessity by natural feminine characteristics, but rather by strong environment forces of education and social tradition under the purposeful control of men."

Women find themselves living in a world where men condemn them to "immanence" and their existence is justified only as objects of sex — "absolute sex, no less". They are defined, as Simone de Beauvoir avers:

> She is simply what man decrees; thus, she is called 'the sex,' by which is meant that she appears essentially to the man as a sexual being. For him she is sex—absolute sex, no less. She is defined and differentiated with reference to man and not he with reference to her, she is the incidental, the inessential, as opposed to the essential He is the subject, he is the Absolute—She is the Other.

Only one thing can help to build a strong character and enhance morality in life that is *yoga.* Vivekananda, a spiritual leader, saint, messenger of Hindu philosophy talks about the various sciences of *yoga.* He gave a new voice and shape to Indian spiritual ideology and travelled across the world to introduce Indian philosophies of *Vedanta* and *yoga* to the Western world. He always had an intellectual quest for God, it was Radhakrishnan who really answered the deep mysteries of Vivekananda. He is known as the exponent of *Raj Yoga, Bhakti Yoga, Jnana Yoga* and *Karma Yoga.* The science of *Yoga* proposes to give us such a means of observing the internal states. The instrument is mind itself. The powers of mind are rays of light dissipated; when they are concentrated, they illumine. This is the only means of knowledge. Since childhood, we are taught to see the external world, but we are never told to peep inside the depth of mind. There is no limit to the power of human mind. The more concentrated it is, the more power is brought to bear on one point, that is the secret. The fire of *Yoga* burns the cage of sin that is around a man. Knowledge becomes purified and *Nirvana* is directly obtained. From *Yoga* comes knowledge; knowledge again helps the *Yogi*. He who combines in himself both *Yoga* and knowledge, with him the Lord is pleased. Here are two Sanskrit words. The one is *Pravritti*, which means revolving towards, and the other is *Nivritti*, which means revolving away. The "revolving towards" is what we call the world, the "I and mine"; it includes all those things which are always enriching that "me" by wealth and money and power, and name and fame, and which are of a grasping nature, always tending to accumulate everything in one centre, that centre being "myself". That is the *Pravritti*, the natural tendency of every human being; taking everything from everywhere and heaping it around one centre, that centre being man's own sweet self. When this tendency begins to break, when it is *Nivritti* or "going away from", then begin morality and religion. Both *Pravritti* and *Nivritti* are of the nature of work: the former is evil work, and the latter is good work.

The man that has practiced control over himself cannot be acted upon by anything outside; there is no more slavery for him. His mind has become free. Such a man alone is fit to live well in the world. We generally find men holding two opinions regarding the world. Some are pessimists and say, "How horrible this world is, how wicked!" Some others are optimists and say, "How beautiful this world is, how wonderful!" To those who have not controlled their own minds, the world is either full of evils or at best a mixture of good and evil. This very world will become to us an optimistic world when we become masters of our own minds." When a man dwells in his mind on the object of sense, attachment to them is produced. From attachment springs desire and from desire comes anger."

"From anger arises bewilderment, from bewilderment loss

of memory; and from loss of memory, the destruction of intelligence and from the destruction of intelligence he perishes." —S. Radhakrishnan, *The Bhagavadgita:*125-26

Many contemporary writers are also exploring spiritual spheres. Literature and music are the expression of life in words of truth and beauty; it is the written record of man's spirit, of his thoughts, emotions, aspirations; it is the history, and the only history, of the human soul. It is characterized by its artistic, its suggestive, and its permanent qualities. Its two tests are its universal interest and its personal style. Its object, aside from the delight it gives us, is to know man, that is, the soul of man rather than his actions; and since, it preserves to the race the ideals upon which all our civilization is founded, it is one of the most important and delightful subjects that can occupy the human mind.

Life is barren without following the spiritual paths of truth and wisdom. The text depicts the contemporary references to the poetry of Bhavabhuti, Bhasa, Kalidasa, Keshava, Rahim, Raskhan, Bihari, Kabir and Meerabai, which also incorporates the aspects of spiritualism, materialism, insolences, politics, metropolitan and rustic scenario. Life is barren without following the spiritual paths of truth and wisdom.

Modernity is making human beings mechanical and materialistic; they are lost in the ocean, struggling to learn the true art of survival. Gandhi wants to get rid of emptiness and meaninglessness of barren life. Gandhi has added all the views and hues of his life to show a path to all the human beings through his unending experiences. Gandhi started writing this book in the dawn of his life and true philosophy of life has been explored. Following Gandhi means understanding one's inner self, realizing oneself, accepting oneself as is, and becoming harmonious with one's surroundings. Spiritual practices should be the important part of human life. Degradation of character and urge for sex without the control upon senses leads to ruin of coming generations. Gandhi constantly urges for the principle of *Brahmacharya*. There is a sound which comes in the form of *Vedas*, Scriptures, *Upanishads*, Couplets, the spiritual poems and Epics, the echoes seem as if coming from distant horizons, they need to be heard, analyzed and observed. Only then the ways of Gandhi can be lived and practiced in real sense.

From Gandhian point of view "*Spirituality is simplicity, sincerity, purity and humility. A simple life helps the seeker grow. A sincere life helps the seeker fly and dive. A pure life helps the seeker become one with God's Vision and God's transcendental Reality. A humble life helps the seeker embrace the length and breadth of the entire world.*"

It is true that Gandhi was actively engaged in dealing with problems that related to the material conditions of life. But he has spared no effort to explain that his activities in the mundane or material fields of life were only meant to serve his spiritual goals, and to prove that even problems that one face in one's day-to-day life could be solved only with means that were consistent with the principles and methods that ruled in the realm of spiritual endeavour. In fact, he claimed that whatever competence or power he had acquired to deal with material conditions and problems had come to him from his spiritual practices.

He rightly said that "... all religions are more or less God-given and ... therefore one must work out one's own salvation in the religion of one's own forefathers; for, a seeker after Truth finds out that all religions melt and become one in God who is one and the same for all His creatures". For Gandhi, the hallmarks of true religion, wherever found, were service and devotion: he robustly insisted that true spirituality, in contrast to outer piety, always resulted in practical work. He said that, "we often prate about spirituality as if it had nothing to do with the ordinary affairs of life and had been reserved for anchorites lost in the Himalayan forest or concealed in some inaccessible Himalayan cave. Spirituality, that has no effect on everyday life is 'an airy nothing'."

Gandhi spoke of God, religion and the spiritual path. But since, these terms have different flavours, he did not want to leave anyone in doubt about his understanding of these words. Gandhi's faith in God was total and unshakable. But to him, God was not a person. Truth and Truth alone was his God. He believed in religion, but to him true religion was not exclusive. It was not a set of catechism and rituals. It was not a hermetically sealed house. He believed that true religion transcended denominations. He believed that those who wanted to tread the spiritual path could not ignore or shun fields of mundane activity. Thus, there was something unique about Gandhi's perception of God, religion and the spiritual faith. Perhaps uniqueness of his perceptions of religion and the spiritual path arose from his perception of God.

The uniqueness of the faith that he chose for his spiritual evolution or self-realization (*Sadhana*) was to attain spiritualism by remaining in the world. The general pattern we have seen is that most of the aspirants renouncing or leaving the world of mundane activity, including himself or herself from the temptations and responsibilities of the mundane world, retiring to the penance grove or the cloister or the wilderness to pursue his spiritual practices, and in some cases, returning after the attainment of self-realization or God-realization to transmit the knowledge or vision that he had come by, or the Gospel that he had heard, to those who were still steeped in the mundane.

Gandhi did not believe in withdrawing from the world of everyday life to devote himself to spiritual practices. To him religion had no meaning and no human activity. In every field he had to look for, and apply the spiritual law. He could not do this if he withdrew from everyday life or the problems or activities of everyday life. If he thought any field was extraneous to the pursuit of the law or truth was not to be followed.

Another unique element in Gandhi's spiritual effort (*Sadhana*) was transparency. He conducted his *'Sadhana'* (spiritual effort) under the gaze of the public. Most of his acts were performed under the watchful eye of the public, with newspapers reporting every move and every reaction. There was nothing hidden from the public nothing that public did not know.

He wrote of his dreams, and examined how far they showed that he had not yet reached where he wanted to reach. These public confessions ensured complete transparency. On the one hand, they ensured that he was not sailing under false colours, dissembling, or benefiting from an untruthful image of himself. On the other, they made common people realize that they could overcome their weaknesses as Gandhi was doing. Gandhi's spiritual effort (*Sadhana*) was therefore unique in that it enabled others to follow every step by which he was struggling to accomplish the ascent. He chose to do his penance in a 'glass-house' watched by others. It could not be otherwise because the God that he was seeking was Truth. Truth did not need secrecy to survive. It was untruth that needed secrecy that needed mask of Truth to survive. Truth and secrecy were therefore antithetical. One who sought Truth could not do so through means that were secret. One could not be truthful without being transparent. Since, transparency was characteristic of the resultant state that he was seeking, the causal method that one adopted had also to be consistent with the character of the resultant state.

Even in early years of his spiritual life in South Africa, he distinguished between formal, denominational or customary religion, and basic or true religion. Explaining his perception, he said, "Let me explain what I mean by religion. It is not the Hindu religion which I certainly prize above all other religions, but the religion which transcends Hinduism, Islam, Christianity and others, which changes one's very nature which binds one indissolubly to the truth within, and which ever purifies. It is the permanent element in human nature which counts no cost too great in order to find full expression and which leaves the soul utterly restless until it has found itself, known its maker, and appreciated the true correspondence between the maker and itself."

"To be true to such religion, one has to lose oneself in the continuing service of all life. Religion or Truth (he equates religion with Truth) is impossible without a complete merging of oneself in or identification with the limitless ocean of life."

If religion is the science of the soul, the quest for Truth, and the pursuit of life that leads one to Truth. What was Gandhi's perception of God? It was the very basis of his life. Gandhi said, "I am sure of His existence than of the fact that you and I are sitting in this room. Then only I can testify that I may live without air and water, but not without Him ... Blast my belief in God, and I am dead."

He came to the conclusion that it would be more correct to say, "Truth is God" than to say "God is Truth. Truth is omnipresent, omnipotent, omniscient."

Gandhi said, "There was a time when I had doubt about existence of God, but **I never doubted the existence of Truth**. This truth is not something material, but pure intelligence. This is for one almost a matter of experience. I have had only a glimpses of it. But my faith is indomitable". Gandhi said, "I do not regard God as a person. Truth for me is God ..."

"To me God is Truth and Love ... He is a personal God to those who need His touch."

Gandhi believed that the power or potential of some *mantras* like *Ramanama* had been identified by spiritual practitioners on the basis of their vision and experience. They were therefore like algebraic formula arrived at through research and experimentation, and verification of effect. Explaining the effect of *namajapa* (repetition of the name), Gandhi says: *Namajapa* cleanse the heart thus: A person who repeats the name with a pure heart does with so with faith. He begins with the resolve that *Namajapa* will purify his heart ... What is on his lips will ultimately possess his heart and purify him. Such experience is universal, and knows no exception. Psychologists are also of opinion that as a man thinks so he becomes. *Ramanama* conforms to this rule. I have firm faith in *Namajapa*. Discovery of *Namajapa* was borne out of experience and understanding and is of utmost importance. The doors of purity should be open even to unlettered, and *namajapa* will unlock them."

If you want to be able to listen to the voice within, you have to be able to silence the deafening and colourous voices of the senses and the ego, and the temptations they offer. There is an indissoluble marriage between matter and spirit. Our ignorance of the results of the union makes it a profound mystery and inspires awe in us, but it cannot undo them. But a living recognition of the union has enabled many to use every physical catastrophe for their own moral uplifting. With me the connection between cosmic phenomenon and human behaviour is a living faith that draws me near to my God (Truth), humbles me and makes me readier for facing him."

The *Gita* talks of the calamity that overtakes humanity and creation when *adharma* (unrighteousness or centrifugal forces) becomes ascendant over *dharma* (righteousness or the centrifugal forces).

This perception of the relation between spirit and matter—or the oneness of spirit and matter may also have contributed to Gandhi's belief that material or physical force could be made to bend before the spiritual force that lay inherent in Truth.

The power of material force may be conditioned by heart which is the seat of comprehension through compassion or feeling. True compassion dissolves the ego, and the dissolution of the ego takes one to a state of consciousness which can be identified only with the realm of the spirit.

Love, to Gandhi, is more than desisting from violence. It is a positive attitude of the mind and heart, and action flowing from that attitude. This attitude does not arise from the moral code laid down by a prophet, or a code that bases itself on the promise of rewards and threats of retribution. It arises from understanding of the unalterable paradigms of human existence. At the basic or gross level, it can be seen that one of the paradigms of human existence is interdependence. When one's existence and achievements are conditioned by interdependence, one has to have positive concern for all others—human beings, other life and the environment—on whom or on which one depends—with whom one's life is interwoven. This concern is love; can be expressed through love. It can neither be expressed through hatred nor indifference. Love is therefore, the *sine qua non* of human existence. It is therefore, according to Gandhi, the force that holds human society together. Since, it is the cohesive force that holds together, it is *Dharma*.

Gandhi believed that love is obverse side of the coin of Truth. Love therefore, cannot acquiesce in the violation of Truth. Love needs to defend truth and it may therefore, confront situations in which it is forced to fight for Truth or serve the cause of Truth through non-cooperation and even disobedience. (Gandhi cites the instance of Prahlad.) Differences do not make enemies of two members of the family.

Spiritual force has no obstructions of the kind that material force has to confront. It can therefore expert its power and achieve results even from a distance, and even without dependence on physical proximity or a material medium. Spiritual force communicates and operates at the spiritual level. It communicates on a trans-physical, trans-verbal, trans-intellectual level with another human being. The experience of such communication becomes possible only when ego-centrism declines and fades.

Love is a spiritual force, and a supremely active and constructive force. It has been already seen that one of the paradigms of human existence is interdependence. Universal love cannot be possessive and suppressive of individuality. It has to be based on human dignity and needs of existence, growth and fulfilment.

Since the fall of Adam and Eve, the devil's strategy is to tempt their descendents thereby destroying their relationship with God (Truth). This is why our attention is often diverted from what is permissible to what is forbidden. Anticipating the pleasure we would receive from forbidden activity, we give in to temptation. The good news is that the devil, our enemy can be disarmed if we concentrate on the things that are permissible, such as exploring the greatness of God, excelling in our respect in trades, building relationships and helping those in need. For, the freedom has so much to offer that we will not have any time to indulge in the forbidden activities. However, this is impossible unless we seek God's strength to fight the devices of the devil.

The world is full of tragedies, events, occurrences and experiences which are meaningless and cruel... We do not need to bow to fatalism. We need not accept the premise that commercial pressures and scientific necessity have the last world. Time and chance may provide the matrix out of which our life flows, but the one who governs all is God. God does throw dice. But that is because we have been born with freedom that allows us to respond to God. We are here to build a kingdom of love with the raw material that we have before us. Sometimes, the raw material we have just decays or cracks or gives way in our hands. But in the seeds of that disintegration, are the beginning of new life.

Gandhiji would not take "philosophy only as ... the thinking consideration of things" as Hegel opines. To him no philosophy that is not useful in life was not acceptable. He courageously stated that he would not accept anything that conflicts with reasons, and conscience. Gandhi's words of wisdom transformed dreams into reality, would have the courage to transform our dreams into reality.

Gandhi believed in the unity of human life, which is a synthetic whole. It cannot be divided into separate, watertight compartments —religious, moral, political, economic, social, individual and collective. Gandhi said, "Drops in separation could only fade away, drops in cooperation made the ocean which carried on its broad bosom ocean greyhounds". Further Gandhi wrote that, "A drop torn from the ocean perished without doing any good. If it remained a part of the ocean, it shared the glory of carrying on its bosom a fleet of mighty steps".

We shall like to conclude that Gandhi's spoken words, writings, and work done by him will resonate for centuries to come. The things that will destroy us are: Politics without principles; Wealth without work; Pleasure without consciences; Knowledge without character; Commerce without morality; Science without humanity; and Worship without sacrifice.

PART TWO
GANDHI ON MORAL BANKRUPTCY

PART TWO

GANDHI ON MORAL BANKRUPTCY

2

TOWARDS MORAL BANKRUPTCY-I

Kind friends continue to send me cuttings from Indian newspapers approvingly dealing with the question of birth-control by the use of contraceptives. My correspondence with young men on their private conduct is increasing. I am able to discuss in these pages only an infinitesimal portion of the questions raised by my correspondents. American friends send me literature on the subject and some are even angry with me for having expressed an opinion against the use of contraceptives. They deplore that, an advanced reformer in many ways, I should be medieval in my views about birth-control. I find too that the advocates of the use of contraceptives number among them some of the soberest of men and women of all lands.

I therefore thought that there must be something very decisive in favour of the methods advocated and felt too that I should say on the subject more than I have done. Whilst I was thinking of the problem and of the question of reading the literature on the subject, a book called *Towards Moral Bankruptcy* was placed in my hands for reading. It deals with this very subject and, as it appears to me, in a perfectly scientific manner. The original is in French by M. Paul Bureau and is entitled *L'Indiscipline des Moeurs* which literally means "the indiscipline of morals". The translation is published by Constable Company and has an introduction by Dr. Mary Scharlieb, C.B.E., M.D., M.S. (Lond.). It covers 538 pages in 15 chapters.

Having read the book, I felt that, before I summarized the author's views, I must in justice to the cause read the standard literature in favour of the methods advocated. I consequently borrowed from the

Servants of India Society such literature as they had on the subject. They have very kindly lent me some of the books in their possession. . . . Kaka Kalelkar who is studying the subject has given me Havelock Ellis's volume specially bearing on the subject and a friend has sent me the special number of *The Practitioner* in which is collected some valuable medical opinion from well-known practitioners.

My purpose in collecting literature on the subject was to test the accuracy, so far as a layman could, of M. Bureau's conclusions. One often finds that there are two sides to questions even when scientists discuss them and that there is much to be said for either side. I was anxious, therefore, to know the viewpoints, of the advocates of contraceptives before I introduced to the reader M. Bureau's volume. I have come to the deliberate conclusion that so far at least as India is concerned, there is no case for the use of contraceptives. Those who advocate their use for Indian conditions either do not know them or choose to ignore them. But if it can be proved that the methods advocated are harmful even in the West, it would be unnecessary to examine the special Indian conditions.

Let us, therefore, see what M. Bureau has to say. His studies are confined to France. But France means much. It is considered to be [one of] the most advanced countries in the world and, if the methods have failed in France, they are not likely to succeed elsewhere.

Opinions may differ as to the meaning of the word 'failure'. I must therefore, define the word as it is here meant. The methods must be proved to have failed if it can be shown that moral bonds have loosened, licentiousness has increased, and, instead of the check having been exercised by men and women for purposes of health and economic limitation of families only, it has been used principally for feeding animal passions. This is the moderate position. The extreme moral position condemns the use of contraceptives under every conceivable circumstance, it being contended that it is not necessary for man or woman to satisfy the sexual instinct except when the act is meant for race reproduction, even as it is not necessary for man or woman to eat except for sustaining the body. There is also the third position. There is a class of men who contend that there is no such thing as morality or that if there is, it consists not in exercising restraint, but in indulgence of every form of animal appetite, so long as it does not so impair the constitution as to render it unfit for the very indulgence which is its object. For this extreme position, I do not suppose, M. Bureau has written his volume. For, M. Bureau concludes his books by quoting Tom Mann's saying: "The future is for the nations who are chaste".

In the first part of his book, M. Bureau has collected facts which make most dismal reading. It shows how vast organizations have sprung up in France which merely pander to man's basest tastes. Even the one claim of advocates of contraceptives that abortions must disappear with the use of these methods cannot be sustained. "It is certain", says M. Bureau, "that during the twenty-five years that have especially seen the increase in France of anti-conceptionist methods, the number of criminal abortions has not become less." M. Bureau is of opinion that abortions are on the increase. He puts down the figure at anything between 2,75,000 and 3,25,000 per year. Public opinion does not look upon them with the horror that it did years ago.

(*Young India,* 1-7-1926)

3

TOWARDS MORAL BANKRUPTCY-II

"In the wake of abortion", says M. Bureau, "come infanticide, incest, and crimes that outrage nature. There is nothing special to say about the first, except that the crime has become more frequent in spite of all the facilities offered to unmarried mothers and of the extension of anti-conceptionist practices and abortion. It no longer arouses the same reprobation among so-called 'respectable' people and juries usually return a verdict of 'not guilty'."

M. Bureau devotes a full section to the growth of pornographic literature. He defines it as the exploitation, with an erotic or obscene intention, of the resources which literature, the drama, and place pictures at men's disposal for their mental refreshment and repose.

And he adds:

In every branch of its business it has secured markets, the extent of which may be gauged by the ingenuity and excellent commercial organization of the directors, the enormous amount of capital, the unexampled perfection of the methods employed . . . The impression has been so strong and so unique that the whole psychological life of the individual is affected by it, a sort of secondary sexual life, which exists wholly in the imagination, is created.

M. Bureau then quotes this pathetic paragraph from M. Ruvsen:

All pornographic and sadistic literature secures in this psychological law the most powerful enticement which it exerts over an innumerable number of readers, and the flourishing circulation of this literature shows beyond dispute that those who live a secondary sexual life through their imagination are legion, not to mention those in lunatic asylums—especially in a period like our own, when the abuse of newspapers and books creates around all consciences what W. James calls "a plurality of under-universe", in which each can lose himself, and forget along with himself the duties of the present hour.

These disastrous consequences, it should never be forgotten, are a direct result of one single fundamental error, namely, that sexual indulgence for its own sake is a human necessity and that without it neither man nor woman reaches their full growth. Immediately a person becomes possessed of such an idea and begins to look upon what in his estimation was one time a vice as a virtue, there is no end to the multiplication of devices that would excite animal passions and help him to indulge in them.

M. Bureau then gives chapter and verse to show how the daily press, the magazine, the pamphlet, the novel, the photograph and the theatre increasingly pander to and provide for this debasing taste.

But the reference hitherto has been to the decay of morals amongst unmarried people. M. Bureau next proceeds to show the measure of moral indiscipline in the married state. He says:

> "Among the aristocracy, the middle class, and the peasants vanity and avarice are responsible for a vast number of marriages. . . . marriage is entered upon also to obtain an advantageous post to join two properties, especially two landed estates, to regularize a former connection or to legitimatize a natural child; to provide unfailing and devoted attentions for a man's rheumatics and old age, to be able to choose the place of his garrison at the time of conscription, Also to put an end to a life of vice, of which they are beginning to weary and to substitute another form of sexual life."

M. Bureau then cites facts and figures to show that these marriages, instead of reducing licentiousness actually promote it. This degradation has been immensely helped by the so-called scientific or mechanical inventions designed to restrict the effect of the sexual act without interfering with the act itself. I must pass by the painful paragraphs regarding the increase in adultery and startling figures regarding judicial separations and divorces which, during the last twenty years, have more than doubled themselves. I can also make only a passing reference to the extension of unrestricted freedom for indulgence to the female sex on the principle of "the same moral standard for the two sexes". The perfection of the anti-conceptional practices and the methods of bringing about abortion have led to the emancipation of either sex from all moral restraint. No wonder marriage itself is laughed at. Here is a passage M. Bureau quotes from a popular author:

Marriage is always according to my judgement one of the most barbarous institutions ever imagined. I have no doubt that it will be abolished if the human race makes any progress towards justice and reason. . . . But men are too gross and women too cowardly to demand a nobler law than that which rules them.

The results of the practices referred to by M. Bureau and of the theories by which the practices are justified are minutely examined.

He explains:

We are, then, being carried away by the movement of moral indiscipline towards new destinies. What are they? Is the future that opens before us one of progress and light, of beauty and growing spirituality, or of retrogression and darkness, of deformity and animalism that is ever demanding more? Is the indiscipline which has been established one of those fruitful revolts against antiquated rules, one of those beneficent rebellions which posterity remembers with gratitude because they were, at certain epochs, the necessary preliminary to its progress and the rise, or is it not rather the old Adam which rises up within us against the rules whose cry strictness is indispensable if we are to withstand the thrust of its bestial appeal? Are we face to face with an evil revolt against the discipline of safety and life?

Then M. Bureau cites overwhelming testimony to show that hitherto the results have been disastrous in every respect. They threaten life itself.

(*Young India,* 8-7-1926)

4
TOWARDS MORAL BANKRUPTCY-III

It is one thing when married people regulate, so far as it is humanly possible, the number of their progeny by moral restraint, and totally another when they do so in spite of sexual indulgence and by means adopted to obviate the result of such indulgence. In the one case, the people gain in every respect. In the other there is nothing, but harm. M. Bureau has produced figures and diagrams to show that the increasing use of contraceptives for the purpose of giving free-play to animal passions and yet obviating the natural results of such indulgence has resulted in the birth-rate being much lower than the death-rate, not in Paris only, but in the whole of France. Out of 87 areas into which France is divided, in 68 the birth-rate is lower than the death rate. In one case, i.e., Lot, deaths were 162 against 100 births. The next comes Tarn-et-Garonne with 156 deaths against 100 births. Even out of 19 areas where the birth rate is higher than the death rate, the difference is negligible in several cases. In ten areas alone is there an effective difference. The lowest death rate, that is 72 against 100 births, occurs in Morbihan and Pas-de-Calais. M. Bureau shows that this process of depopulation, which he calls 'voluntary death', has not yet been arrested.

M. Bureau then examines the condition of French Provinces in detail and he quotes the following paragraph from M. Gide written in 1914, about Normandy:

Normandy has lost in the course of 50 years more than 3,00,000 inhabitants, that is to say, a population equal to that of the whole department of the Orne. Every 20 years she now loses the equivalent of a department, and as she includes but five, a century will be enough to see her fat meadows empty of Frenchmen—I say advisedly of Frenchmen, for assuredly others will come to occupy them, and it would be a pity were it otherwise. Germans work the iron mines round Caen, and for the first time, only yesterday, a vanguard of Chinese labourers landed where William the Conqueror set sail for England.

And M. Bureau adds by way of comment on the paragraph,

How many other provinces are in no better condition!

He then goes on to show that this deterioration in population has inevitably led to the deterioration in the military strength of the nation. He believes that the cessation of emigration from France is also due to the same cause. He then traces to the same cause the decay of French communal expansion, the decay of French commerce and the French language and culture.

M. Bureau then asks:

Are the French people who have rejected the ancient sexual discipline more advanced in securing happiness, material prosperity, physical health, and in intellectual culture?

He answers:

With regard to the improvement in health, a few words will suffice. However, strong our wish to answer all objections methodically, it is all the same very difficult to take seriously the assertion that sexual emancipation, would tend to strengthen one's body and improve one's health. On every side one hears of the diminished vigour of both, young people and adults. Before the war the military authorities had to lower, time after time, the physical standard of the recruits, and the power of endurance has seriously diminished throughout the whole nation. Doubtless it would be unjust to maintain that lack of moral discipline is alone responsible for this decline, but it has a large share in it, together with alcoholism, insanitary housing, etc.; and if we look closely we shall easily discover that this indiscipline and the sentiments which perpetuate it are the strongest allies of these other scourges. . . . The frightful extension of venereal diseases has done incalculable injury to the public health.

M. Bureau even disputes the theory advanced by Neo-

Malthusians that the wealth of individuals in a society which regulates its births increases in proportion to the restriction it imposes upon them, and fortifies his answer by comparing the favourable German birth-rate and her increasing material prosperity with the decreasing birth-rate of France side by side with its decreasing wealth. Nor has the phenomenal expansion of German trade, M. Bureau contends, been attained at the cost of the German workmen more than elsewhere. He quotes M. Rossignol:

People died of hunger in Germany when she had but 4,10,00,000 inhabitants: they have become richer and richer since she numbered 6,80,00,000.

And adds:

These people, who are by no means ascetic, found it possible to place annually in the savings-banks sums which in 1911 amounted to 22,000 million francs; while in 1895 the deposits only reached 8,000 millions, an increase of 850 millions a year.

The following paragraph which M. Bureau writes after describing the technical progress of Germans about the general culture will be read with much interest:

Without being initiated into the depths of sociology one can have no doubt of it, for it is quite evident, that such technical progress would have been impossible had not workmen of a more refined type, foreman more highly educated perfectly trained engineers been found. . . . The Industrial schools are of three kinds: professional, numbering over 500, with 70,000 pupils; technical, still more numerous, and some of them with over 1,000 pupils; lastly, the colleges devoted to higher instruction with their 15,000 pupils, which confer, like the Universities, the envied title of doctor . . . 365 commercial schools attract 31,000 pupils and in innumerable schools courses of agriculture give instruction to over 90,000. What, compared with these 4,00,000 pupils in the different lines of the production of wealth, are the 35,000 pupils of our professional courses, and why, since 17,70,000 of our people, of whom 7,79,798 are below eighteen years of age, live by the cultivation of the soil, are there but 3,225 pupils in our special schools of agriculture?

M. Bureau is careful enough to note that all this phenomenal rise of Germany is not entirely due to the surplus of births over deaths, but he does contend with justice that, given other favourable conditions, a preponderating birth rate is an indispensable condition of national growth. Indeed, the proposition he has set forth to prove is that a growing birth rate is in no way inconsistent with great material prosperity and moral progress. We in India are not in the position of France so far as our birth rate is concerned. But it may be said that the preponderating birth rate in India, unlike as in Germany, is no advantage to our national growth. But I must not anticipate the chapter that will have to be set apart for a consideration of Indian conditions in the light of M. Bureau's facts and figures and conclusions.

After dealing with an examination of German conditions where birth rate preponderates the death rate, M. Bureau says:

Are we not aware that France occupies the fourth place–and that a very long way below the third–in regard to the total sum of national wealth? France has an annual revenue from her investments of 25,000 million francs, while the Germans are drawing from their investments a revenue estimated at 50,000 million francs.... Our national soil has suffered in thirty five years, from 1879 to 1914, a depreciation of 40,000 million Francs, and is worth only 52,000 instead of 92,000 millions! Whole departments of the country lack men to work the soil, and there are districts where one sees scarcely any but old men.

He adds that:

Moral indiscipline and systematic sterility means the diminution of natural abilities in the community, and the undisputed predominance of the old men in social life. . . . In France, there are but 170 children and young people to every 1,000 inhabitants, while, in Germany, there are 220, in England, 210. . . . The proportion of the old is greater than it should be and the others who are prematurely aged through moral indiscipline and voluntary sterility share in all the senile fears of a debilitated race.

The author then observes:

We know that the immense majority of French people are indifferent to this domestic position (slack morals) of their rulers, thanks to the convenient theory of the "wall round private life".

And he quotes with sorrow the following observation of M. Leopold Monod:

It is a fine thing to go to war in order to cast down infamous abuses, and to break the chains of those who we suffer from them. But how about men whose fears have not known how to guard their consciences from enticements; men whose courage is at the mercy of a caress or a fit of sulks; . . . men who with no shame, perhaps glorying in the exploit, repudiate the vow which in a joyous and solemn hour they made to the wife of their youth; men who burden their home with the tyranny of an exaggerated and selfish egotism—how can such men be liberators?

The author then sums up:

Thus, whichever way we turn, we always find that the various forms of our moral indiscipline have caused serious hurt to the individual, the family, and society at large, and have inflicted on us suffering which is literally inexpressible. The licentious conduct of our young people, prostitution, pornography, and marriages for money, vanity or luxury, adultery and divorce, voluntary sterility and abortion, have debilitated the nation and stopped its increase; the individual has been unable to conserve his energies, and the quality of the new growth has diminished simultaneously with its quantity.

"Fewer births and more fine men" was the watchword, which had something enticing about it for those who, shut-up in their materialistic conception of individual and social life, thought they could assimilate the breeding of men to that of sheep or horses. As Auguste Comte said with stinging force, these pretended physians of our social ills would have done better to become veterinary surgeons, incapable as they always were of comprehending the infinite complexity of the psychology both of the individual and of the society.

The truth is that of all the attitudes which a man adopts, of all the decisions, at which he arrives, of all the habits which he contracts, there is none which exerts over his personal and social life an influence comparable to that exerted by his attitudes, his decisions, and his habits with regard to the appeals of the sexual appetite. Whether he resists and controls them, or whether he yields and allows himself to be controlled by them, the most remote regions of social life will experience the echo of his action, since nature has ordained that the most hidden and intimate action should produce infinite repercussions.

Thanks to this very mystery, we like to persuade ourselves, when we violate in any way the moral discipline, that our misdeed will have no grievous consequence. As to ourselves, in the first place, we are satisfied, since our own interest or pleasure has been the motive of our action; as to society at large, we think it is so high above our modest selves that it will not even notice our misdeeds; and, above all, we secretly hope that "the others" will have the sense to remain devout and virtuous. The worst of it is that this cowardly calculation almost succeeds while our conduct is as yet an abnormal and exceptional act; then, proud of our success, we persevere in our attitude, and when there is occasion we come—and this is our supreme punishment—to believe it lawful.

But a day comes when the example given by this conduct involves other defections; each of our evil deeds has the result of making more difficult and more heroic that attachment to virtue which we have counted on in "the others", and our neighbour, tired of being duped, is now in a hurry to imitate us. That day the downfall begins and each can estimate at once the consequences of his misdeeds and the extent of his responsibilities. . . .

The secret act has come out of the hiding-place in which we thought it was confined. Endowed in its own way with a kind of immaterial radio-activity, it has run through all sections; all suffer from the fault of each, action, like the wavelets spreading from an eddy, makes itself felt in the most remote regions of the general social life. . . .

Moral indiscipline at once dries-up the fountains of the race, and hastens the wear and tear of the adults whom it debilitates both morally and physically.

(*Young India,* 15-7-1926)

5
TOWARDS MORAL BANKRUPTCY-IV

Having dealt with the indiscipline of morals and its aggravation by the use of contraceptives and its terrible results, the author M. Bureau proceeds to examine the remedies. I must pass over the portions that deal with legislative measures, their necessity and yet utter inefficiency. He then discusses the necessity, by a careful education of public opinion of the duty of chastity for the married, the duty of marriage for that vast mass of mankind that cannot for ever restrain their animal passions, the duty, having once married, of conjugal fidelity and the duty of continence in marriage. He examines the argument against chastity that its precept is against the physiological nature of man and woman and injurious to the happy equilibrium of their health.

That it is an intolerable attack on the freedom and autonomy of the individual, his right to happiness and to live his life is his own way.

The author contests the doctrine that "the organ of generation is like the "rest" requiring satisfaction." He says,

> "If it were an organ like the others, how could we explain the absolute inhibitory power which the will possesses over it? Or the fact that the awakening of sensuality, which pharisaism calls the sexual necessity, is the result of the innumerable excitements which our civilization provides for young boys and girls several years before normal adult age?"

I cannot resist the temptation of copying the following valuable medical testimony collected in the book in support of the proposition that self-restraint is not only not harmful, but necessary for the promotion of health and perfectly possible:

"The sexual instinct", says Esterlen, professor at Tubigen University, "is not so blindly all-powerful that it cannot be controlled, and even subjugated entirely, by moral strength and reason. The young man, like the young woman, should learn to control himself until the proper time. He must know that robust health and ever renewed vigour will be the reward of this voluntary sacrifice.

> "One cannot repeat too often that abstinence and the most absolute purity are perfectly compatible with the laws of physiology and morality, and that sexual indulgence is no more justified by physiology and psychology than by morality and religion."

"The example of the best and noblest among men", says Sir Lionel Beale, professor at the Royal College in London, "has at times proved that the most imperious of instincts can be effectively resisted by a strong and serious will, and by sufficient care as to manner of life and occupation. Sexual abstinence has never yet hurt any man when it has been observed, not only through exterior restrictive causes", but as a voluntary rule of conduct.

Virginity, in fine, is not too hard to observe "provided that it is the physical expression of a certain state of mind. . . . Chastity implies not only continence, but also purity of sentiments, the energy which is the result of deep convictions."

"Every kind of nervous activity", says the Swiss psychologist Forel, who discusses sexual anomalies with a moderation equal to his knowledge, "is increased and strengthened by exercise. On the other hand, inactivity in a particular region reduces the effects of the exciting causes which correspond to it."

> "All causes of sexual disturbance increase the intensity of desire. By avoiding these provocations it becomes less sensitive and the desire gradually diminishes. The idea is current among young people that continence is something abnormal and impossible, and yet the many who observe it prove that chastity can be practised without prejudice to the health."

"I know", says Ribbing, "a number of men of 25, 30, and older than that, who have observed perfect continence, or who when they married had done so up to that time. Such cases are not rare; only they do not advertise themselves."

"I have received many confidences from students, healthy both in body and mind" who have remonstrated with me for not having sufficiently insisted on the ease with which sensual desires can be ruled."

"Before marriage, absolute continence can and ought to be observed by young men", says Dr. Acton. "Chastity no more injures the body than the soul", declares Sir James Paget, Physician to the English Court; "Discipline is better than any other line of conduct."

"It is a singularly false notion", writes Dr. E. Perier, "and one which must be fought against, since, it besets not only the children's mind, but that of the fathers as well: the notion of imaginary dangers in absolute continence. Virginity is a physical, moral, and intellectual safeguard to young men."

"Continence", says Sir Andrew Clarke, "does no harm, it does not hinder development, it increases energy and enlivens perception. Incontinence weakens self-control, creates habits of slackness, dulls and degrades the whole being, and lays it open to diseases which can be transmitted to several generations. To say that incontinence is necessary to the health of young men is not only an error, but a cruelty. It is at once false and hurtful."

"The evils of incontinence are well-known and undisputed", writes Dr. Surbled: "those produced by continence are imaginary; what proves this is the fact of the many learned and voluminous works devoted to the explanation of the former, while the latter still await their historian. As to these latter there are but vague assertions, which hide themselves, for very shame, in mere talk, but which will not endure the daylight."

"I have never seen", writes Dr. Montegazza in *La Physiologie de l'amour,* "a disease produced by chastity.... All men, and especially young men, can experience the immediate benefits of chastity."

Dr. Dubois, the famous professor of neuropathology at Berne, affirms that "there are more victims of neurasthenia among those who give free rein to their sensuality than among those who know how to escape from the yoke of mere animalism"; and his witness is fully confirmed by that of Dr. Fere, Physician at the Bicetre Hospital, who testifies that those who are capable of psychic chastity can maintain their continence without any fear of their health, which does not depend on the satisfaction of the sexual instinct.

"There has been unfitting and light talk", writes Professor Alfred Fournier, "about the dangers of continence for the young men. I can assure you that if these dangers exist I know nothing about them, and that as a physician I am still without proof of their existence, though I have had every opportunity in the way of subjects under my professional observation.

"Besides this, as physiologist I will add that true virility is not attained before the age of twenty-one, or thereabouts, and the sexual necessity does not obtrude itself before that period, especially if unhealthy excitements have not aroused it prematurely. Sexual precocity is merely artificial, and is most often the result of ill-directed upbringing.

"In any case, be sure that danger of this kind lies far less in restraining than in anticipating the natural tendency; you know what I mean."

Lastly, after these most authoritative testimonies, to which it be easy to add many others, let us quote the resolution unanimously voted at Brussels in 1902 by the 102 members present at the second General Congress of the International Conference of Sanitary and Moral Prophylaxis, a congress which assembled together the most competent authorities on the subject throughout the world: "Young men must above all be taught that chastity and continence are not only not harmful, but also that these virtues are among those to be most earnestly recommended from the purely medical and hygienic standpoint."

There was also a unanimous declaration issued by the professors of the Medical Faculty of Christian University, a few years ago: "The assertion that a chaste life will be prejudicial to the health rests, according to our unanimous experience on no foundation. We have no knowledge of any harm resulting from a pure and moral life."

The case has, therefore, been heard, and sociologists and moralists can repeat with M. Ruysen this elementary and physiological truth, "that the sexual appetite does not need, like the requirements of ailment and exercise, a minimum of necessary satisfaction. It is a fact that man or woman can lead a chaste life without experiencing, except in the case of a few abnormal subjects, serious disturbance or even painful inconvenience. It has been said and cannot be too often repeated, since, such an elementary truth can be so widely disregarded—that no disease ever comes through continence to normal subjects, who form the immense majority while many diseases, very well known and very serious, are the results of incontinence. Nature has provided in the most simple and infallible way for the excess of nutrition which is represented by the seminal fluid and the menstrual flux."

Dr. Viry is therefore right in denying that the question is one of a true instinct or a real need: "Everyone knows what it would cost him not to satisfy the need of nourishment or to suppress respiration, but no one quotes any pathological consequences, either acute or chronic, as having followed either temporary or absolute continence. . . . In normal life we see the example of chaste men who are neither less virile in character, nor less energetic in will, nor less robust, than others, nor less fitted to become fathers if they marry. . . . A need which can be subject to such variations, an instinct which accommodates itself so well to lack of satisfaction, is neither a need nor an instinct."

Sexual relationship is far from answering to any physiological need of the growing boy; quite the contrary, it is perfect chastity which is sternly required by the exigencies of his normal growth and development, and those who violate it cause irreparable injury to their health. The attainment of puberty is accompanied by great changes, a veritable disturbance of various functions, and a general development. The adolescent boy needs all his vital strength, for during this period there is often a weakening of the resistance to sickness: disease and mortality are higher than in the earlier period . . . The long work of general growth of organic evolution, that whole series of physical and psychic changes, at the end of which the child becomes a man, involves a toilsome effort of nature. At that moment, all over-driving is dangerous, but especially the premature exercise of the sexual function.

(*Young India*, 22-7-1926)

6
TOWARDS MORAL BANKRUPTCY-V

After dealing with the physiological benefit of chastity, M. Bureau quotes the following passage from Professor Montegazza on its moral and intellectual advantages:

"All men, and young men in particular, can experience the immediate benefit of chastity. The memory is quiet and tenacious, the brain lively and fertile, the will energetic, the whole character gains a strength of which libertines have no conception; no prism shows us our surroundings under such heavenly colours as that of chastity, which lights up with its rays the least objects in the universe, and transports us into the purest joys of an abiding happiness that knows neither shadow nor decline." And the author adds: "The joy, the cordial merriment, the sunny confidence of vigorous young men who have remained chaste . . . are an eloquent contrast to the restless obsessions and feverish excitement of their companions who are slaves to the demands of sensuality." He then compares the benefits of chastity with "the miserable consequences of lust and debauchery". "No disease", the author states, "could ever be quoted as the result of continence; who is not aware of the frightful diseases of which moral indiscipline is the source?" "The body . . . finds itself converted into an indescribable state of rottenness. . . . Nor can we forget the worse defilement of imagination, heart and understanding. On every side we hear complaint of the lowering of the character, the unbridled lust of youth, the overflowing of selfishness."

So much for the so-called necessity of sexual indulgence and the consequent liberty taken by the youth before marriage. The protagonists of the doctrine of such indulgence further contend that restraint of the sexual passion is a restraint upon "the freedom to dispose of one's body". The author shows by elaborate argument that restraint on individual freedom in the matter of sexual indulgence is a sociological and psychological necessity. The author says,

"In the eyes of sociologists, social life is nothing but a net-work of multiform relations, nothing, but an interlacing of actions and reactions, in the midst of which an activity, isolated and really separated from the rest, is unthinkable.

On whatever step we resolve, whatever action we attempt, solidarity unites our resolution and our action to those of our brothers; and not even our most secret thought or most fugitive wish fails of an echo so distant that the mind is for ever incapable of measuring the distance. The social quality is not, in man, an adventitious or merely accessory quality: it is immanent, part of his humanity itself; he is a social being because he is a man. There is no other field of our activity so truly our own: physiology and morality, economics and politics, the intellectual and aesthetic domains, the religious and the social, all are conditioned by a universal system of mysterious bonds and undefined relations. The bond is so firm, the net so closely meshed, that sometimes the sociologist stands in real trouble before this immensity which unfolds itself before him, across all time and space; he measures in one glance how great, under certain circumstances, is the responsibility of the individual, and how he risks becoming petty by a liberty which some social circles might be tempted to grant him."

The author further says,

"If we can say that under certain circumstances I am not at liberty to spit in the street . . . how can I claim the much more important right of disposing of my sexual energy as I like? Does that energy by a unique privilege escape the universal law of solidarity? Who does not see, on the contrary, that the sovereign importance of the function only increases the social reaction of the individual acts? Look at this young man and this girl who have just established that false union of which the reader knows the character; they are persuaded that the agreement concerns nobody, but themselves. They shut themselves up in their independence, and pretend to believe that their intimate and secret action has no interest for society and is altogether beyond its control. A childish illusion! The social solidarity which unites the people of one nation, and, beyond the individual nations, all humanity, finds no difficulty in passing through all walls, even those of the secret chambers, and a terrible interrelation joins that supposed private action to the most distant series of actions in that social life which it helps to disorganize. Whether he wills it or not, every individual who asserts his right to temporary or sterile sexual relations, who claims the liberty to use the reproductive energy with which he is endowed merely for his own enjoyments, spreads in society the germs of division and disorder. All, deformed as they are by our selfishness and our disloyalties, our social institutions still take for granted that the individual will accept with goodwill the obligations inherent in the satisfaction of the reproductive appetite. It is by discounting this acceptance that society has built-up its countless mechanisms of labour and property, of wages and inheritance, of taxation and military service, of the right of parliamentary suffrage and civil liberties. By his refusal to: take his share the individual disorganizes everything at one stroke, he violates the social pact in its very essence, and while he makes the burden heavier on others' shoulder, he is no better than an exploiter and a parasite, a thief and a swindler. We are responsible in the face of society for our physiological energy, as for all our energies, and, it might be said, even more than for all the others, since a society unarmed and almost wholly without external pressure, is obliged to remit to our goodwill the care to use that energy judiciously, and conformably to the social good."

The author is equally strong on the psychological ground:

It was said long ago that liberty is in appearance an alleviation, in reality a burden. That is precisely its grandeur. Liberty binds and compels; it increases the sum of the efforts which each is bound to make. The individual desires to be free, he is all inflamed with the longing to realize himself in the expansion of his autonomy. The programme seems simple enough, and yet his first experiences are enough to show him its painful complexity. It is in vain that unity is the dominating characteristic of our nature and our moral life, we feel within us various and contradictory impulses; in each of them we are conscious of ourselves, and yet everything proves to us that we must choose between them. You say, young man, that you wish to live your own life, to realize yourself, we ask with the great pedagogue, Foerster: Which is the better part, that which has its seat in the centre of your intellectual force, or that which occupies the lowest, the sensual, part of your nature? If it is true that progress in the individual and in society consists in a growing spiritualization and in the ever more complete mastery of spirit over matter, the choice cannot be doubtful, but there must still be energy to act, and the undertaking is not an easy one. Perhaps you will reply: But I do not choose. I wish to realize my being in one harmonious and organized whole. Very well; but take care this very resolution is a choice, for harmony is only established at the cost of strife. *Sterbe und Wade,* die and become, said Goethe, and the words are but the echo of others spoken nineteen centuries ago by Christ, "Amen, I say to you, unless the grain of wheat falling into the ground die, it remaineth alone; but if it die, it bringeth forth much fruit."

"We wish to be men—an easy thing to say", writes Mr. Gabriel Seailles, "but the right turns into duty, stern duty, in which no one does not fail more or less; we wish to be free, we announce it with a menacing air; if we call liberty doing as we like, the slavery of instinct; we need not be so proud of it; if we are speaking of the true liberty, let us gird up our loins and prepare ourselves for the unending fight. We talk about our unity, our identity, our liberty, and proudly conclude that we are immortal sons of God. Alas! if we only try to seize this Self, it escapes our grasp, it resolves itself into a multitude of incoherent beings which deny each other, it is rent by contradictory desires which in turn constitute itself, it is wholly (its own essential being excepted) the prejudice to which it submits, the objects which tempt it; its pretended liberty is nothing, but a slavery which does not feel, so does not resist.

"While continence is a virtue full of repose, incontinence opens the door to an unknown guest who may become formidable. The revelation of passion, which is troublesome at any age, may become in youth the signal of a radical perversion, we would say of an irreparable disturbance of the balance of the will and the senses. The boy who has contact for the first time with any woman whatsoever, as a passing encounter, is really playing with his physical, intellectual, and moral life; he does not know, but it will be the same tomorrow in the family, at work, in social life; he does not know how the sensual revelation will come back to haunt him, what servitude without hope may represent the too exact term of 'mastery'; and we know of more than one life ruined after a beginning of richest promise, the first disappointments of which dated from the first moral fall."

The celebrated verses of the poet echo these remarks of the philosopher:

> Man's virgin soul is as a vessel deep;
> If the first drops inpoured should tainted be.
> Across the soul all ocean's waves may sweep,
> Yet fail that vast abyss from stain to free.

And, not less, this advice of the great British physiologist, John G. M. Kendrick, Professor of Physiology at Glasgow University:

> "The illicit satisfaction of nascent passion is not only a moral fault, it is a terrible injury to the body. The new need becomes a tyrant if yielded to; a guilty complacency will listen to it, and make it more imperious; every fresh act will forge a new link in the chain of habit."
>
> "Many have no longer strength to break it, and helplessly end in physical and intellectual ruin, slaves of a habit contracted often through ignorance rather than perversity. The best safeguard consists in cultivating within oneself purity of thought and discipline of one's whole being."

M. Bureau adds to the foregoing the following from Dr. Franck:

> "As to sexual desire, we assert that the intelligence and the will have absolute control over it. It is necessary to employ the term *sexual desire,* not *need,* for there is no question of a function, the non-accomplishment of which is incompatible

wish existence. Really, it is not a need at all; but many men are persuaded that it is. The interpretation they give to the desires makes them look on co-habitation as absolutely necessary. Now, we cannot look on the sexual act as resulting from senile and passive obedience to natural laws; we are, on the contrary, concerned with a voluntary act, following on a determination or an acquiescence, often premeditated and prepared for."

(*Young India,* 29-7-1926)

7
TOWARDS MORAL BANKRUPTCY-VI

After having insisted on chastity before and during marriage and shown by overwhelming proof that not only is self-restraint not impossible, not harmful, but perfectly possible and wholly beneficial both to the mind and the body, M. Bureau devotes a chapter to the value and possibility of perpetual continence. The following opening paragraph is worth reproducing:

In the first rank of these liberators, these heroes of the true sexual emancipation, it is only right to name the young men and women who, the better to devote themselves to the service of a great cause, choose to remain all their life in chastity, and renounce the joys of marriage. The reasons for their resolve vary according to circumstances: one feels it a duty to remain with an infirm father or mother; another takes the place, to orphaned brother and sisters, of the departed parents; another desires to devote himself or herself entirely to the service of science or art, of the poor or the sick, or to a work of moral education or of prayer. Similarly, the merit of the voluntary sacrifice may be greater or less; some, thanks to the benefits of a wise protective education and the practice of a good moral hygiene, are almost without sensual temptations; other, more advanced in the path of virtue, have succeeded, it may be at the cost of sharp conflicts of which they alone know the hardness, in mastering the beast and taming the flesh. On any supposition, the final resolve is the same: the men and women have been led to think that the best way for them to serve is not to marry; and they have entered into an engagement, it may be with themselves, it may be with God, to remain in the perfect chastity of the celibate life. However, definite and undoubted may be the duty of marriage, as we shall see under certain circumstances, all these resolutions are legitimate, because they are inspired by a noble and generous purpose." Painting is a jealous mistress who suffers no rival", replied Michael Angelo when marriage was suggested to him; and how many after him have had a like experience!

I can corroborate this testimony from the experience of European friends of almost every description given by M. Bureau, friends who exercised perpetual restraint. It is only in India that from childhood we must hear of marriages. Parents have no other thought, no other ambition save that of seeing their children well married and provided for. The one thing brings premature decay of mind and body and the other induces idleness and often makes of one a parasite. We exaggerate the difficulty of chastity and voluntary poverty and impute extraordinary merit to them, reserve them for *mahatmas* and *yogis* and rule the latter out of ordinary life, forgetting that real *mahatmaship* and *yoga* are unthinkable in a society where the ordinary level is brought down to the mudbank. On the principle that evil, like the hare, travels faster than good which like the tortoise, though steady, goes slow, voluptuousness of the West comes to us with lightning speed and with all its variegated enchantment dazzles and blinds us to the realities of life. We are almost ashamed of chastity and are in danger of looking upon self-imposed poverty as a crime in the fate of the Western splendour that descends upon us from minute to minute through the cable and day to day through the steamers that discharge their cargo on our shores. But the West is not wholly what we see in India. Even as the South African Whites ill-judge us when they judge us through the Indian settlers, so shall we ill-judge the West through the human and the other Western cargo that delivers itself to us every day. There is in the West a small but inexhaustible reservoir of purity and strength which those who have eyes of penetration may see beneath the deceptive surface. Throughout the European desert, there are oases from which those who will may drink the purest water of life. Chastity and voluntary poverty are adopted without brag, without bluster, and in all humility by hundreds of men and women, often for no other than the all sufficing cause of service of some dear one or of the country. We often prate about spirituality as if it had nothing to do with the ordinary affairs of life and had been reserved for anchorites lost in the Himalayan forests or concealed in some inaccessible Himalayan cave. Spirituality that has no bearing on and produces no effect on everyday life is "an airy nothing". Let young men and women for whose sake *Young India* is written from week to week know that it is their duty if they would purify the atmosphere about them and shed their weakness, to be and remain chaste and know too that it is not so difficult as they have been taught to imagine.

Let us further listen to M. Bureau:

In proportion as it (modern sociology) follows the evolution of our manners, and as methodical study digs more deeply the soil of social realities, the better is the value perceived of the help which the practice of perpetual chastity brings to the great work of the discipline of the senses. . . . If marriage is the normal state of life for the immense majority of people, it cannot be that all can, or ought to marry. Even putting aside the exceptional vocations of which we have just spoken, there are at least three classes of celibates who cannot be blamed for not being married: the young people of both sexes who for professional or economic reasons think it a duty to defer their marriage; the people who are involuntarily condemned to celibacy because they cannot find a suitable partner; finally, those who ought to abstain from marriage in consequence of their physiological defects that could be transmitted, and in some who are strictly bound to renounce all idea of it. Is it not evident, then, that the renunciation made by these people, doubly necessary both for their own happiness and the interests of society, will be rendered so much the less painful and so much the more cheerful, because they will find beside them others who, in full possession of their physical and intellectual vigour and sometimes with abundant means have declared their firm resolution to remain celibate all their lives? These voluntary and choice celibates, who have willed to consecrate themselves to God without reserve, to prayer and to the training of the souls, declare that in their eyes celibacy, far from being a reduced condition of life, is on the contrary a superior state, in which man asserts, in its plenitude, the mastery of the will over instinct.

The author says:

To young people of both the sexes, who are still too young to marry perpetual cilibacy shows that it is possible to pass one's youth chastely; to the married it recalls the duty which lies upon them to maintain exact discipline in their conjugal discipline and never to allow a consideration of self-interest however legitimate it be in itself, to prevail over the higher demands of moral generosity.

Foerster says:

The vow of the voluntary celibate far from degrading marriage, is on the contrary the best support of the sanctity of the conjugal bond, since it represents in a concrete form man's freedom in the face of the pressure of his nature. It acts like a conscience with regard to passing whims and sensual assault. Celibacy is also a protection to marriage in the sense that its existence prevents married people from looking upon themselves in their mutual relations as mere slaves to obscure natural forces, and it leads them to take openly in the face of nature, the position of free beings who are capable of mastery. Those who scoff at perpetual celibacy as unnatural or impossible do not know really what they are doing. They fail to see that the line of thought which makes them talk as they do must necessarily lead, by strict logic, to prostitution and polygamy. If the demand of nature is irresistible, how can a chaste life be required of married people? And lastly, they forget the great number of marriages in which, it may be for several months or years, or even for life, one of the spouses is condemned to a real celibacy by the sickness or other disability of the partner. For this reason alone, true monogamy rises or falls with the esteem that is paid to celibacy.

(*Young India,* 5-8-1926)

8
TOWARDS MORAL BANKRUPTCY-VII

The chapter on perpetual continence is followed by chapters on the duty and indissolubility of marriage. Whilst the author contends that perpetual continence is the highest state, it is not possible for the multitude for whom marriage must be regarded as a duty. He shows if the function and limitations of marriage are rightly understood, there never can be any advocacy of contraceptives. It is the wrong moral training that has brought about the prevalent moral indiscipline.

Having dealt with the opinion of 'advanced' writers ridiculing marriage the author says:

Happily for future generations, this opinion of pseudo moralists and of writers who are often utterly lacking in moral sense, and equally so sometimes in the real literary spirit, is very far from being that of the true psychologists and sociologists of our time; and in nothing is the rupture more complete between the noisy world of the press, the novel, and the stage, and that other world where thought is cultivated, and the mysterious elements of our psychological and social life are studied in detail.

M. Bureau rejects the argument of free love. He holds that "marriage is the union of man and woman, the association for life, the communication of divine and human rights of law". Marriage is not a "mere civil contract" but a sacrament, a "moral obligation". It has succeeded in" making the gorilla stand erect".

It is a great mistake to imagine that everything is permissible to those lawfully married and even supposing that husband and wife ordinarily respect the moral law as to transmission of life, it is untrue that it is lawful to *add* other modes of sexual intercourse which please them. This prohibition is as much in their interest as in that of society of which their marriage ought to be the maintenance and development.

The author holds that:

"The ever renewed opportunities of deviation from strict discipline which marriage affords to the sexual instinct are a constant menace to true love. This peril can only be exorcised by watchfulness to keep the satisfaction of the sexual appetite within the limits defined by the very ends of marriage."

"It is always dangerous", says St. Francis of Sales, "to take to violent medicines since if one takes more than should be taken, or if they are not well made up, much harm is done; marriage has been blessed and ordained partly as a remedy for concupiscence, and it is undoubtedly a very good remedy, but all the same a violent one, and consequently very dangerous if not discreetly used."

The author then combats the theory of individual liberty to contract or break the marriage bond at will or to live frankly a life of indulgence without its consequent obligation. He insists on monogamy and says:

"It is untrue that the individual is at liberty to contract marriage or to remain in selfish celibacy, as he pleases; still less are duly married people free to agree together to the rupture of their union. Their freedom is shown when they choose each other, and each is bound to choose only with full knowledge, after careful thought, the one with whom he believes he can assume the responsibilities of the new life he is entering. But as soon as the marriage has been accomplished and consummated, the act performed involves, far away and in all directions, incalculable consequences which extend infinitely beyond the two persons who have brought them about. These consequences may be unperceived, in a time of anarchic individualism such as ours, by the spouses themselves, but their importance is certified by the grave sufferings which come upon the whole body social, as soon as the stability of the home is shaken, as soon as the variable caprice of the sensual appetite takes the place of the beneficent discipline of the positive monogamic union. To one who is conscious of these indefinitely extended repercussions and these subtle connections, it matters little to know that, since all human institutions are subject to the universal law of evolution, that of marriage must certainly, like all the rest, undergo in its turn necessary transformations, since, there can be no doubt that progress in this direction can only take the form of eventually drawing more closely the marriage bond. The attacks now made on the rule of the indissolubility of marriage "when divorce is asked for by mutual consent" will only bring into more prominent relief the social value of a rule against which protest is made, and as the years roll by this rule, which for some centuries, when its social value could not yet be appreciated, was simply a prescription of religious discipline, will appear more and more as a principle as beneficial to the individual as it is salutary for society at large.

The rule of indissolubility is not an arbitrary adornment; on the contrary, it is bound-up with the most delicate mechanism of the individual and collective social life; and since people talk about evolution, they should ask on what condition this indefinite progress of the race which all agree to desire, is possible. The deepening of the sense of responsibility, the training of the individual towards autonomous discipline willingly consented to, the growth of patience and charity, the control of selfishness, the maintenance of the emotional life against the elements that make for dissolution and the impulse of passing caprice—all these are dements in man's interior life which we are entitled to consider the absolute and permanent conditions of all higher social culture, and on this account exempt from all such disorder as might result from a serious change in economic conditions. To tell the truth, economic progress is itself closely bound up with general social progress, for economic security and success depend in the long run on the sincerity and loyalty of our social co-operation. Every economic modification which ignores these fundamental conditions is self-condemned. If we wish, therefore, to take up the study, at once both moral and social, of the absolute value of the various methods of sexual relations, the following question is decisive: What method is the best adapted to the deepening and strengthening of our whole social life? Which is the most capable, at the different periods of life, of developing to the utmost the sense of responsibility, self-abnegation and sacrifice, of most effectively restraining undisciplined selfishness and capricious frivolity? When the matter is viewed from this standpoint, there is not the slightest doubt that monogamy, because of its social and educative value, must form part of the permanent heritage of all more advanced civilizations; and true progress will draw more closely, rather than relax, the marriage bond. . . . The family is the centre of all human preparation for the social life, that is to say, all preparation for responsibility, sympathy, self-control, mutual tolerance, and reciprocal training. And the family only fills this central place because it lasts all through life and is indissoluble, and because, thanks to this permanence, the common family life becomes deeper, more stable, more adapted to men's mutual intercourse than any other. It may be said that monogamic marriage is the conscience of all human social life."

He quotes Auguste Comte: "Our hearts are so changeable that society must intervene to hold in check the vacillation and caprices which would otherwise drag down human existence to be nothing but a series of non-worthy and pointless experiences. Satisfaction of lust is never the end of marriage."

"A fiction", writes Dr. Toulouse, "which often hinders the happiness of married people, is that the instinct of love is a tyrant and must be satisfied at any price . . . Now, the very characteristic quality of man, and the apparent end of his evolution" is an ever growing independence of his appetites. The child learns to master his coarser needs, and the adult to overcome his passions. This scheme of all good upbringing is not chimerical, nor something outside practical life for the end of our nature is precisely to be subject, in great degree, to the personal tendencies which constitute our will. What one shelters behind as 'temperament' is usually nothing but weakness. The man who is really strong knows how to use his powers at the right time."

(*Young India,* 12-8-1926)

9

TOWARDS MORAL BANKRUPTCY-VIII

It is now time to conclude this series of articles. It is not necessary to pursue M. Bureau in his examination of the doctrine of Malthus who startled his generation by his theory of overpopulation and his advocacy of birth-control if the human species was not to be extinct. Malthus, however, advocated continence, whereas Neo-Malthusianism advocates not restraint, but the use of chemical and mechanical means to avoid the consequences of animal indulgence.

M. Bureau heartily accepts the doctrine of birth-control by moral means, i.e., self-restraint, and, as we have seen, rejects and vigorously condemns the use of chemical or mechanical means. The author then examines the condition of working classes and the proportion of birth among them and finally closes the book by examining the means of checking the practice of grossest immoralities under the name of individual freedom and even humanity. He suggests organized attempt to guide and regulate the public opinion and advocates State interference, but finally relies upon quickening of the religious life.

Moral bankruptcy cannot be met or arrested by ordinary methods, most certainly not when immorality is claimed as a virtue and morality condemned as a weakness, superstition or even immorality. For many advocates of contraceptives do indeed condemn continence as unnecessary and even harmful. In this state of things religious aid is the only effective check upon licensed vice. Religion here may not be taken in its narrow, parochial sense. True religion is the greatest disturbing factor in life, whether individual or collective. A religious awakening constitutes a revolution, a transformation, a regeneration.

And nothing but some such dynamic force can positively prevent the moral catastrophe towards which, in M. Bureau's estimation, France seems to be moving.

But we must here leave the author and his book; French conditions are not Indian conditions. Ours is a somewhat different problem. Contraceptives are not universal in India. Their use has hardly touched the educated classes. The use of contraceptives in India is, in my opinion, unwarranted by any single condition that can be named. Do middle class parents suffer from too many children? Individual instances will not suffice to make out a case for excessive birth rate among the middle classes. The cases in India where I have observed the advocacy of these methods are those of widows and young wives. Thus, in the one case it is illegitimate birth that is to be avoided, not the secret intercourse. In the other, it is again pregnancy that is to be feared, and not the rape, of a girl of tender age. Then there remains the class of diseased weak effeminate young men who would indulge in excesses with their own wives or others' wives and would avoid the consequences of acts which they know to be sinful.

The cases of men or women in full vigour of life desiring intercourse and yet wishing to avoid the burden of children are, I make bold to say, rare in this ocean of Indian humanity. Let them not parade their cases to justify and advocate a practice that in India, if it became general, is bound to ruin the youth of the country. A highly artificial education has robbed the nation's youth of physical and mental vigour. We are offspring in many cases of child-marriages. Our disregard of the laws of health and sanitation has undermined our bodies. Our wrong and deficient dietary composed of corroding spices has produced a collapse of the digestive apparatus. We need, not lessons in the use of contraceptives and helps to our being able to satisfy our animal appetite, but continuous lessons to restrain that appetite, in many cases even to the extent of absolute continence. We need to be taught by precept and example that continence is perfectly possible and imperatively necessary if we are not to remain mentally and physically weak. We need to be told from the housetop that if we will not be a nation of manikins, we must conserve and add to the limited vital energy we are daily dissipating. Our young widows need to be told not to sin secretly, but come out boldly and openly to demand marriage which is their right as much as that of young widowers. We need to cultivate public opinion that shall make child marriages impossible. The vacillation, and the disinclination to do hard and sustained work, the physical inability to perform strenuous labours, collapses of enterprises brilliantly begun, the want of originality, one notices so often, are due largely to excessive indulgence. I hope young men do not deceive themselves into the belief that, when there is no procreation, the mere indulgence does not matter, does not weaken. Indeed the sexual act, with the unnatural safeguard against procreation, is likely to be far more exhausting than such act performed with a full sense of the responsibility attached to it.

The mind is its own place, and in itself Can make a heaven of hell, a hell of heaven. If we begin to believe that indulgence in animal passion is necessary, harmless and sinless, we shall want to give reins to it and shall be powerless to resist it. Whereas, if we educate ourselves to believe that such indulgence is harmful, sinful, unnecessary and can be controlled, we shall discover that self-restraint is perfectly possible.

Let us beware of the strong wine of libertinism that the intoxicated West sends us under the guise of new truth and so-called human freedom. Let us, on the contrary, listen to the sober voice from the West, that through the rich experience of its wise men at times percolates to us, i.e. if we have outgrown the ancient wisdom of our forefathers.

Charlie Andrews has sent me an informing article on "Generation and Regeneration" written by William Loftus Hare and printed in *The Open Court* (March 1926). It is a closely-reasoned scientific essay. He shows that all bodies perform two functions: "namely, internal reproduction for the building-up of the body and external reproduction for the continuance of the species." These processes he names regeneration and generation, respectively.

The regenerative process—internal reproduction—is fundamental for the individual and, therefore, necessary and primary; "the generative process is due to a superfluity of cells and is therefore secondary .... The law of life, then, at this level is to feed the germ cells, firstly, for regeneration, and, secondly, for generation. In case of deficiency, regeneration must take the first place and generation be suspended. Thus, we may learn the origin of the suspension of reproduction and follow it to its later phases of human continence and asceticism generally. Inner re-production can never be suspended except at the cost of death, the normal origin of which is thus also discerned."

After describing the biological process of regeneration the writer states:

"Among civilized human beings sexual intercourse is practised vastly more than is necessary for the production of the next generation and is carried on at the expense of internal reproduction, bringing disease, death and more in its train."

No one who knows anything of Hindu philosophy can have difficulty in following this paragraph from Mr. Hare's essay:

"The process of regeneration is not and cannot be mechanistic in character, but like the primitive fission, is vitalistic. That is to say, it exhibits intelligence and will. To suppose that life separates, differentiates and segregates by a process that is purely mechanistic is inconceivable. True, these fundamental processes are so far removed from our present consciousness as to seem to be uncontrolled by the human or animal will. But a moment's reflection will show that just as the will of the fully developed human being directs his external movements and actions in accordance with the guidance of the intellect—this, indeed, being its function so the earlier processes of the gradual organization of the body must, within the limits provided by environment be allowed to be directed by a kind of will guided by a kind of intelligence. This is now known to psychologists as 'the unconscious'."

It is a part of ourself, disconnected from our normal daily thinking, but intensely awake and regard in regard to its own functions—so much so that it never for a moment subsides into sleep as the consciousness does.

Who can measure the almost irreparable harm done to the unconscious and more permanent part of our being by the sexual act indulged for its own sake?

The nemesis of reproduction is death. The sexual act is essentially katabolic (or a movement towards death) in the male and in parturition of the offspring it is katabolic for the female.

Hence, the writer contends:

"Virility, vitality and immunity from disease are the normal lot of nearly or quite continent persons. Withdrawal of germ cells from their upward regenerative course for generative or merely indulgent purposes deprives the organs of their replenishing stock of life, to their cost slowly and ultimately.

It is these physical facts which constitute the basis of a personal sexual ethic, counselling moderation, if not restraint—at any rate, explaining the origin of restraint."

The author, as can be easily imagined, is opposed to birth-control by chemical and mechanical means. He says:

"It removes all prudential motives for self-restraint and makes it possible for sexual indulgence in marriage to be limited only by the diminution of desire or the advance of old age. Apart from this, however, it inevitably has an influence outside the marriage relation. It opens the door for irregular, promiscuous and unfruitful unions, which from the point of view of modern industry, sociology and politics, are full of danger. I cannot go into these here. It is sufficient to say that by contraception, inordinate sexual indulgence both in and out of marriage is facilitated and, if I am right in my foregoing physiological arguments, evil must come to both individuals and the race."

Let the Indian youth treasure in their hearts the quotation with which M. Bureau's book ends:

"The future is for the nations who are chaste."

(*Young India,* 19-8-1926)

APPENDEX

1. CURING SEX OBSESSION

It is desirable that every man and woman should carefully study the translation published in this issue of the substance of the new book [1] on marriage written by an author named Thurston. Among us, starting from boys of the age of fifteen right-up to men of fifty or, in the case of girls, starting from an even younger age up to women of fifty, the belief is current that it is not possible to live without the gratification of our sexual desires. Hence, both the sexes are in a continuous state of excitement. They do not trust each other and a man changes colour when he sees a woman and *vice versa.* Because of this, certain customs have become prevalent, as a result of which both men and women have lost their vitality and have become sickly and listless and our lives have been reduced to a state which is unworthy of human beings.

Even in the *Shastras* which came into being in such an atmosphere, such commands and beliefs are found which result in a man and a woman having to act as if they were enemies of each other.

This is so because sexual desires are aroused or there is a fear of their being aroused when a member of either sex catches a glimpse of a member of the other sex.

Because of this belief and because of the customs that have been forged on the basis of this belief, one's life is spent in the gratification of sexual desire or in thinking about it, with the result that life becomes as bitter as poison.

As a matter of fact, because, of his powers of discretion, man should have greater strength for renunciation and should be able to exercise more self-control than animals. Despite this, it is our everyday experience that man fails to observe the limits observed by animals in their relationship with members of the opposite sex. Ordinarily, the relationship between a man and a woman should be similar to that between a mother and a son, a sister and a brother or a father and a daughter. It is obvious that the relationship between husband and wife can be something in the nature only of an exception, and a man would be afraid of being with a woman and *vice versa* only if a brother and a sister need be thus afraid. On the contrary, in actual practice even the relationship between a brother and a sister is not free from inhibitions. And they are taught to cultivate such inhibitions.

It is absolutely necessary to save ourselves from this pitiable condition, that is, from this atmosphere polluted by sexual desire. The ignorant fear that we cannot free ourselves from this has taken deep root in us. True manliness lies in destroying it, and we should acquire the confidence that it is possible to do.

Thurston's little book helps greatly in such an effort. I for one feel that this writer's theory—that, at the root of this desire are the current beliefs regarding marriage and the customs, both in the East and in the West, based on them—is correct. For a man and a woman to sleep alone at night in one room and share a bed between them is fatal to both and is a potent means of universalizing the reign of sexual desire and making it permanent. For religious preachers and reformers to preach self-control when all married couples behave like this, is like trying to patch up the sky. It is not surprising that the measures adopted for practising self-control are futile in an atmosphere where sex is so predominant. The *Shastras* proclaim that the sexual desire should be indulged in only for the purpose of procreation. This commandment is being violated every moment and yet people look for other causes for the resulting diseases. This is an action similar to that of a person who, while carrying his child on his hips, searches for it in the whole town. If this fact which is clear as daylight is understood, we would do the following:

1. Men and women would take a pledge today that they would not sleep in privacy and would not engage in procreation without mutual consent. Whenever possible, they should sleep in separate rooms. Where this is not possible due to poverty, they should sleep on separate beds, set far apart, and have some friend or relation to sleep between them.
2. Understanding parents should not give their daughter in marriage unless she is going to be provided with a separate room and a separate bed. Marriage is a kind of friendship. A man and a woman become partners in joys and sorrows, so

> that as soon as they are married, on the very first night they should not give in to the gratification of their sexual desire and lay the foundation of the ruin of their lives. Children should be given such training.

The new, wonderful beneficent and peaceful conception that is implied in the acceptance of Thurston's theory deserves to be pondered over and it is necessary to understand the changes that ought to be made in the prevalent ideas on marriage. We can profit from this discovery only if this can take place. If those who have been able to understand this discovery have children of their own, they should accordingly alter their children's education and the atmosphere in their own homes.

We should not require Thurston's testimony or his support in order to realize the harmful nature of the tremendous propaganda that is being carried on at present for the use of artificial methods of birth-control side by side with the gratification of sexual desire. It is surprising how this method can be adopted in India at all. It passes my understanding how educated persons suggest this method in the prevalent enervating atmosphere in this country.

[From Gujarati]

(*Navajivan,* 30-9-1928)

2. SEXUAL PERVERSION

Some years ago, the Bihar Government in its education department had an inquiry into the question of unnatural vice in its schools, and the Committee of Inquiry had found the existence of the vice even among teachers who were abusing their position among their boys in order to satisfy their unnatural lust. The Director of Education had issued a circular prescribing departmental action on such vice being found to exist in connection with any teacher. It would be interesting to know the results, if any, issuing from the circular.

I have had literature too sent to me from other provinces inviting my attention to such vice and showing that it was on the increase practically all-over India in public as well as private schools.

Personal letters received from boys have confirmed the

information. Unnatural though the vice is, it has come down to us from times immemorial. The remedy for all secret vice is most difficult to find.

And it becomes still more difficult when it affects guardians of boys which the teachers are. "If the salt loses its savour, wherewith shall it be salted?" In my opinion departmental action, necessary as it is in all proved cases, can hardly meet the case. The levelling-up of public opinion alone can cope with the evil. But in most matters there is no such thing as effective public opinion in this country. The feeling of helplessness that pervades political life has affected all other departments. We therefore pass by many a wrong that is being perpetrated in front of us.

3. SEX EDUCATION[2]

Sjt. Maganbhai Desai, who received the other day the degree equivalent to Master of Arts from the Gujarat Vidyapith, wrote to me a Gujarati letter dated 7th October from which I cull the following:[3]

> May I invite you to discuss in the columns of *Harijanbandhu* a question which you have so far left more or less untouched, I mean the question of imparting sex instruction to young people? . . .
>
> Should sex education be included in the educational curricula of our children? Who should impart it? What would be the necessary qualification for the task? Should this subject be taught in a matter-of-fact manner to all and sundry just like geography or arithmetic? Or is there any limit? And if so, who is to draw the line and where? Again, should the aim of sex education be to combat the onset of libido or simply to recognize it as an inevitable fact of nature which has to be accepted and submitted to?
>
> May I also take leave to make a special request in this connection? Apart from what you may write on this subject in English, would not you write something for the Gujarati reader in Gujarati? You know it is an old-standing grievance of ours that you have ceased to give your original contributions in Gujarati. . . .

I kept this letter for such a long time hoping that one day I should write something on the subject discussed in it. Meanwhile, I had to go to Ahmedabad to preside at the Twelfth Gujarati Sahitya Parishad.[4] During my stay of four days at the Vidyapith and in course of contact with Gujarati men and women there, past incidents came afresh to me. I was confronted by the man who had gently castigated me in the above mentioned letter. He even asked me, "What about that letter?" I pacified him by saying that I was carrying it everywhere with me and that I would definitely write about it. At that time I wanted to write in English. On reaching Segaon, I felt the impact of Maganbhai's castigation. I was reminded of the bitter but affectionate quarrel with Swami Anand in the days of *Navajivan.* He could not bear that I should contribute my original ideas to *Young India* while only stale versions should go to *Navajivan.* I also felt the same. Yet my insistence on writing in *Young India* was not out of place. I think at long last Swami Anand got tired and stopped troubling me. Even after the lapse of such a long time I cannot say definitely which of us two was right. Be it as it may, having said this much by way of introduction I wish to tell the readers of *Harijanbandhu* that I fully agree with Shri Maganbhai's complaint. And from now onwards, every week I will try to give something new to the Gujarati readers. I appeal to them to encourage me in my effort.[5]

Preoccupation with sex is daily becoming more marked in Gujarat as in the rest of India. And what is more, those who fall under its sway feel as if there is something meritorious about it. When a slave begins to take pride in his fetters and hugs them like precious ornaments, the triumph of the slave-owner is complete. But this success of Cupid, spectacular though it may be, will, I am convinced, prove to be short-lived and ignoble, and at long last end in inanition even like a scorpion whose venom is spent. But that does not mean that we can in the meantime afford to sit with folded hands. The certainty of its defeat need not, must not, lull us into a false sense of security. The conquest of lust is the highest endeavour of a man's or a woman's existence. Without overcoming lust man cannot hope to rule over self. And without rule over self there can be no *Swaraj* or *Ramarajya.* Rule of all without rule of oneself would prove to be as deceptive and disappointing as a painted toy mango, charming to look at outwardly, but hollow and empty within. No worker who has not overcome lust can hope to render any genuine service to the cause of *Harijans*, communal unity, *khadi*, cow-protection or village reconstruction. Great causes like these cannot be served by intellectual equipment alone, they call for spiritual effort or soul-force. Soul-force comes only through God's grace, and God's grace never descends upon a man who is a slave to lust.

What place has then instruction in sexual science in our educational system, or has it any place there at all? Sexual science is of two kinds, that which is used for controlling or overcoming the sexual passion and that which is used to stimulate and feed it.

Instruction in the former is as necessary a part of a child's education as the latter is harmful and dangerous and fit therefore only to be shunned. All great religions have rightly regarded *Kama* as the archenemy of man, anger or hatred coming only in the second place.

According to the *Gita*, the latter is an offspring of the former. The *Gita* of course uses the word *kama* in its wider sense of desire. But the same holds good of the narrow sense in which it is used here.

This, however, still leaves unanswered the question, viz., whether it is desirable to impart to young pupils a knowledge about the use and function of generative organs. It seems to me that it is necessary to impart such knowledge to a certain extent. At present they are often left to pick up such knowledge anyhow, with the result that they are misled into abusive practices. We cannot properly control or conquer the sexual passion by turning a blind eye to it. I am therefore strongly in favour of teaching young boys and girls the significance and right use of their generative organs. And in my own way, I have tried to impart this knowledge to young children of both sexes for whose training I was responsible.

But the sex education that I stand for must have for its object the conquest and sublimation of the sex passion. Such education should automatically serve to bring home to children the essential distinction between man and brute, to make them realize that it is man's special privilege and pride to be gifted with the faculties of head and heart both; that he is a thinking, no less than a feeling, animal, as the very derivation of the word *manushya* shows, and to renounce the sovereignty of reason over the blind instincts is therefore to renounce a man's estate. In man reason quickens and guides the feeling, in brute the soul lies over dormant. To awaken the heart is to awaken the dormant soul, to awaken reason, and to inculcate discrimination between good and evil.

Who should teach this true science of sex? Clearly, he who has attained mastery over his passions. To teach astronomy and kindred sciences we have teachers who have gone through a course of training in them and are masters of their art. Even so must we have as teachers of sexual science, i.e., the science of sex control, those who have studied it and have acquired mastery over self. Even a lofty utterance that has not the backing of sincerity and experience will be inert and lifeless, and will utterly fail to penetrate and quicken the hearts of men, while the speech that springs from self-realization and genuine experience is always fruitful.

Today our entire environment—our reading, our thinking, our social behaviour—is generally calculated to subserve and cater for the sex urge. To break through its coils is no easy task. But it is a task worthy of our highest endeavour. Even if there are a handful of teachers endowed with practical experience, who accept the ideal of attaining self-control as the highest duty of man, are fired by a genuine and undying faith in their mission, and are sleeplessly vigilant and active, their labour will light the path of the children of Gujarat, save the unwary from falling into the mire of sexuality and rescue those who might be already engulfed in it.

(*Harijan*, 21-11-1936, and *Harijanbandhu*, 22-11-1936)

Notes

1. *Thurston's Philosophy of Marriage; vide* "Startling Conclusions", 27-9-1928.
2. Translated from Gujarati by Pyarelal. The original appeared in *Harijanbandhu*, 22-11-1936.
3. Only extracts have been reproduced here.
4. *Vide* "Speech at Gujarati Sahitya Parishad", 31-10-1936 and "Speech at the Concluding Session of the Twelfth Gujarati Sahitya Parishad, Ahmedabad", 2-11-1936.
5. This paragraph has been taken from *Harijanbandhu*.

Bibliography

Andrews, C.F., 1949. *Mahatma Gandhi's Ideas*, London: George Allen & Unwin Ltd.

Andrews, C.F., 1931. *Mahatma Gandhi at Work Ideas*, London: George Allen & Unwin Ltd.

Appadorai, A., 1981. *Documents on Political Thought in Modern India*, Vol. 1, New Delhi: Oxford University Press.

Bandyopadhyaya, J., 1969. *Social and Political Thought of Gandhi*, Calcutta: Allied Publishers, Calcutta.

Bhattacharyya, Buddhadeva, 1969. *Evolution of Political Thought of Gandhi*, Calcutta: Calcutta Book House.

Birla, G.D., 1953. *In the Shadow of the Mahatma*, Bombay: Orient Longmans Ltd.

Bondurant, Joan, 1959. *Conquest of Violence: The Gandhian Philosophy of Conflict*, Bombay: Oxford University Press.

Bose, Anima, 1987. *Dimensions of Peace and Non-violence: The Gandhian Perspective*, New Delhi: Gian Publishing House.

Bose, N.K., 1962: *Studies in Gandhism*, Ahmedabad: Navajivan Publishing House.

Bose, N.K., 1966. *Gandhiji: The Man and His Mission*, Bombay: Bharatiya. Vidya Bhawan.

Bose, N.K., 1972. *Selections from Gandhi*, Ahmedabad: Navajivan Publishing House.

Brown, Judith M., 1977. *Gandhi and Civil-Disobedience*, London: Cambridge University Press.

Brown, Judith M., 1972. *Gandhi's Rise to Power, Indian Politics*, 1915-22, London: Cambridge University Press.

Brown, M. Judith, 1992. *Gandhi Prisoner of Hope*, Delhi: Oxford University Press.

Chatterjee, Margaret, 1992. *Gandhi's Religious Thought*, London.

Chopra, Pran, 1972. *The Sage in Rivolt: A Remembrance*, New Delhi: Gandhi Peace Foundation.

Choudhuri, Manmohan, 1987. *Exploring Gandhi*, New Delhi: The Gandhi Peace Foundation.

Datta, D.M., 1953. *The Philosophy of Mahatma Gandhi*, Madison: University of Wisconsin Press, 1953.

Doke, J.J., 1909. *M.K. Gandhi: An Indian Patriot*, Madras: Natesan.

Erikson, Erik H., 1970. *Gandhi's Truth: On the Origins of Militant Non-violence*, London: Faber and Faber Limited.

Fischer, Louis, 1962. *The Essential Gandhi*, London: George Allen & Union Limited.

Gandhi, M.K., 1988. *An Autobiography or the Story of My Experiments With Truth*, Ahmedabad: Navajivan Publishing House.

Gandhi, M.K., 1975: *Hind Swaraj or Indian Home Rule*, Ahmedabad: Navajivan Publishing House.

Gandhi, M.K., 1975. *Satyagraha in South Africa*, Ahmedabad: Navajivan Publishing House.

Gandhi, Rajmohan, 2006. *Mohandas: A True Story of a Man, his People and an Empire*, New Delhi: Penguin.

Gandhi, Rajmohan, 1995. *The Good Boatman: A Portrait of Gandhi*, New Delhi: Penguin Books.

Gregg, Richard B., 1960. *The Power of Non-Violence*, Ahmedabad: Navajivan Publishing House.

Green, Martin, 1993. *Gandhi: Voice of a New Age Revolution*, New York: Continuum.

Guha, Ramachandra, 2008. *India After Gandhi: The History of the World's Largest Democracy*, New Delhi: Picador.

Hardiman, David, 2003. *Gandhi: In His Time and Ours*, New Delhi: Permanent Black.

Holmes, J.H.; Bridge, P.C. and James, F.E., *Mahatma Gandhi: World Significance*, Calcutta: C.C. Basik, The Research Home.

Hunter, Doris A. and Mallick Krishna, 1990. *Non-violence: A Reader in the Ethics of Action*, New Delhi: Gandhi Peace Foundation.

Huttenback, Robert A., 1971. *Gandhi in South Africa: British Imperialism and the Indian Question, 1860-1914*, London: Cornell University Press.

Huxley, A., 1937. *Ends and Means*, London: Kegan Paul.

Iyer, Raghavan, 1973. Chicago: *The Moral and Political Thought of Mahatma Gandhi*, Oxford University Press.

Jack, A. Homer (Ed.), 1984. *The Gandhi Reader*, Madras: Samata Books.

Kripalani, J.B., 1968. *Gandhi: His Life and Thought*, New Delhi: Publications Division, Ministry of Information and Broadcasting, Government of India.

Mishra, Anil Dutta, 2012. *Reading Gandhi*, New Delhi: Pearson.

Mishra, Anil Dutta, 2011. *Understanding Mahatma Gandhi: Speeches and Writings that Reveal his Mind Methods and Mission*, New Delhi: Concept Publishing Co. (P) Ltd.

Mishra, Anil Dutta, *et al.*, 2011. *Revisiting Gandhi*, New Delhi: Abhijeet Publications.

Mishra, Anil Dutta, 2010. *Mahatma on Ethics*, New Delhi: Concept Publishing Co. (P) Ltd.

Mishra Anil Dutta, 2010. *Revisiting Hind Swaraj*, New Delhi: Concept Publishing Co. (P) Ltd.

Mishra, A.D. (ed.), 2002. *Perspectives on Human Rights*, New Delhi: Radha Publications.

Mishra, Anil Dutta (Ed.), 1996. *Gandhian Approach to Contemporary Problems*, New Delhi: Mittal Publications.

Mishra, Anil Dutta and M.S. Dadage, 2000. *Panchayati Raj: Gandhian Perspective*, New Delhi: Mittal Publications.

Mishra, Anil Dutta, 2003. Challenges of *21st Century and Gandhian Alternative*, New Delhi: Mittal Publications.

Mishra, Anil Dutta, 1995. *Fundamentals of Gandhism*, New Delhi: Mittal Publications.

Mishra, Anil Dutta, 2002. *Rediscovering Gandhi*, New Delhi: Mittal Publications.

Mishra, Anil Dutta, 1996. *Gandhian Approach to Contemporary Problems*, New Delhi: Mittal Publications.

Mishra, Anil Dutta, 1999. *Gandhism After Gandhi*, New Delhi: Mittal Publications.

Mukerjee, Hiren, 1960. *Gandhi: A Study*, New Delhi: People's Publishing House.

Namboodiripad, E.M.S., 1959. *The Mahatma and the Ism*, New Delhi: People Publishing House.

Nanda, B.R., 1959. *Mahatma Gandhi: A Biography*, London: George Allen & Unwin Ltd.

Narayan, Shriman, 1956. *Selected Works of Mahatma Gandhi*, Ahmedabad: Navajivan Publishing House.

Nehru, Jawahar Lal, 1949. *Mahatma Gandhi*, Calcutta: Signet Press.

Ostergaord Geoffrey, 1985. *Non-violent Revolution in India*, New Delhi: Gandhi Peace Foundation.

Parekh, Bhikhu, 1989. *Colonialism, Tradition and Reform: An Analysis of Gandhi's Political Discourse*, New Delhi: Sage Publications.

Parel, Anthony J., 2006. *Gandhi's Philosophy and the Quest for Harmony*, Cambridge: Cambridge University Press.

Polak, H.S.C., H.N. Brailsford and Lord Pethick, Lawrence, 1949. *Mahatma Gandhi*, London: Odham Press Limited.

Prabhu, R.K., and Rao, U.R., 1967. *The Mind of Mahatma*, Ahmedabad: Navajivan Publishing House.

Pyare Lal, 1956, 1958. *Mahatma Gandhi: The Early Phase*, Volume 1, Ahmedabad: Navajivan Publishing House, 1965.

Pyare Lal, 1956, 1958. *Mahatma Gandhi: The Last Phase*, in 2 volumes, Ahmedabad: Navajivan Publishing House.

Pyarelal and Nayar Sushila, 1991. *In Gandhiji's Mirror*, New Delhi: Oxford University Press.

Pyarelal, 1958. *Mahatma Gandhi, The Last Phase*, Ahmedabad: Navajivan Publishing House.

Radhakrishnan, S. (Ed.), 1961. *Mahatma Gandhi: Essays and Reflections on His Life and Thought*, Allahabad: Kitabistan.

Radhakrishnan, S. (Ed.), 1968. *Mahatma Gandhi 100 Years*, New Delhi: Gandhi Peace Foundation.

Rajendra Prashad, 1961. *At the Feet of Mahatma Gandhi*, Bombay: Asia Publishing House.

Rao, U.R., 1963. *The Way to Communal Harmony*, Ahmedabad: Navajivan Publishing House.

Rao, U.S. Mohan (Ed.), 1968. *The Message of Mahatma Gandhi*, New Delhi: Publication Division, Ministry of Information and Broadcasting, Government of India.

Sharp, Gene, 1960. *Gandhi Wields the Weapon of Moral Power Three Case Histories*, Ahmedabad: Navajivan Publishing House.

Sharp, Gene, 1973. *The Politics of Non-Violent Action: Power and Struggle*, Part 1, Boston: Porter Sarget Publishers.

Sheean Vincent, 1990. *Mahatma Gandhi: A Great Life in Brief*, New Delhi: Publication Division.

Shukla, Chandrashanker, 1951. *Reminiscences of Gandhiji*, Bombay: Vora & Company.

Sitaramayya, Pattabhi, 1942. *Gandhi and Gandhism*, in 2 volumes. Allahabad: Kitabistan.

Tendulkar, D.G., 1952. *Mahatma*, New Delhi: Publications Division, Ministry of Information and Broadcasting, Government of India.

Watson, Francis and Tennyson Hallam, 1957. *Talking of Gandhi*, Bombay: Sangam Books.

Weber, Thomas, 1991. *Conflict Resolution and Gandhian Ethics*, New Delhi: The Gandhi Peace Foundation.

Weber, Thomas, 1997. *On the Salt March*, New Delhi: Harper Colliings.

Weber, Thomas, 2004. Gandhi: *As Disciple and Mentor*, New Delhi: Cambridge University Press.

Index